He's A man of Love
He bought me at a high price,
He paid my dowry.
He is coming back for me
because Love is patient and
Love is Loyal, I can wait.

Beautiful Love, How Great!

What manner of man!

Betty Amiina

Published by PublishingPush.com

Contents

The prayer

Powerful and Mighty, God, you have the whole world in your hands: In 2012, while planning this book I wrote this prayer, it was titled, ***prayer for the whole world*!** Our heavenly Father, King of glory, we thank you. We worship you, we glorify you and we honour you because no one can love us like you do. We thank you Jesus. You are a wonderful Saviour. Saviour of the world you died on the cross to save us. Giver of life we praise your holy name. Heavenly Father forgive our sins, because we know that you have the power to forgive us. Also let **us** forgive those who offend us because in the Gospel of *Matthew while teaching us to pray we are told that* if we can't forgive them that hurt us, you will not forgive us. *The Lord's prayer: our Father who is in heaven. Hallowed be your name.*

Your Kingdom come, your will be done on Earth as it is done in heaven.

Give us this day our daily bread. ***And forgive us our sin/debts as we forgive we forgive those who sin against us. (as we forgive our debtors.)*** *Do not lead us into temptation.*

But deliver us from the evil one, for yours is the Kingdom

An the power and the glory forever, Amen, Matthew 6: 9-13.

Father we pray that you provide to us our needs, give us love to love one another and to be kind to one another. To help one another, to be fair and to treat others with respect, and to walk in your ways. Jesus, you are the best example. You are the light of the world and those who walk with you cannot see darkness, *John 8:12, I'm the light of the world, he who follows me will not walk in darkness but have the light of life.* Father, let your light shine in everything we do: in our speech and also in our walk, if we have the light of God in us everything we do will be different then our Father in heaven we be glorified. *Matthew 5:16, Let your light so shine before men, that they may see your good works and give glory to your Father in heaven.* Father Lord teach us to be humble and *to be* polite, you hate arrogance and those who walk in pride you abase. For we know that pride leads to destruction. Help us not to be proud of those things which do not bring any glory to your name. We ask that you cover the whole world with the blood of Jesus, yes, we know that there is power in that blood. Mighty God, King of king, Greater I am, Master of the Universe, Powerful Saviour, we bless your name. Almighty God save us from the hands of satan and all his agents, in the Mighty name of Jesus we have prayed, Amen.

***Eight years ago**, when my life was beautiful in some ways, I wrote this letter to God.*

To *my Friend in heaven my Lord and my Shepherd:*

Dear God, thank you for being so good. You are a true Father, friend and Saviour. You died on the cross because of my sins. Jesus, I worship you, I give you all the glory there is no none like you. Jehovah Shammah, Ever present God, you will never leave me nor forsake me. You are the rock of my strength, and my salvation. I will never deny you Jesus, King of glory, my Navigator I praise you. You mend a broken heart even when it is shattered you put it together. Nothing is impossible with you, that is why I call you, impossible doer. You are a merciful God. You don't want the people you created to perish but to have everlasting life. Father save us from the king of the darkness and bring us to your light. We want to see clearly where we are going, we do not want to fall into the pit. Father Lord we know that your home is in heaven and you will come back to receive those who are ready to go with you. You said in the gospel of *John 14: 6, I'm the way, the truth and life, no one comes to the Father except through me.* Those who believe in you will live forever: *John 11:25, Jesus said, "I am the resurrection and life: he who believes in me, though he dies he shall live.* You give life, those who are ready to receive it will have it. Those who are ready go with you will have life externally, hell fire will is not see us because it's you that we want, we want follow you.

Praise God.

I found love

Amazing love, how sweet: His love is kind, His love is patient and His love so generous! Bible says, *John 3:16, for God so loved the world that He gave His only begotten son, that whoever believes in Him should not perish but have everlasting life.* I received a short song, amazing love; *amazing love, amazing love, amazing love of Jesus,*

Jesus you love me, Jesus you love me,
Jesus you love so much!
Jesus you love me so much!
Amazing love, amazing love, amazing love of Jesus.

In this the love of God was manifested towards us (me) that God sent His only begotten son into the world that we might live through Him,1 John 4:9.

1 John 4:14, we have seen and testify that the Father has sent the Son as Saviour of the world.

What man of love is this! *Behold what manner of love the Father has bestowed on us that we should be called children of God,1John 3v1.*

1 John 3:16, by this we know ***love*** *because He laid down His life for us. And* ***we*** *also out to lay* ***down*** *our* ***lives*** *for the* ***brethren****.*

1 John 4:11, beloved if God so loved us, we ought to love one another.

A love so wonderful! Back in Uganda we sing a song which says,

Jesus' love is very wonderful, Jesus' love is very wonderful, Jesus' love is very wonderful, oh what a wonderful love. So high you can't get over it, so high you can't get over it, so high you can't get over it, oh what a wonderful love!

Spending time writing songs, one day I came up with a song titled, *there is a man I love, He is so wonderful to me, His love is so wonderful, His love is so beautiful, His love so precious and so sweet. Do you know the love I'm talking about, I'm talking about the love of Jesus. Jesus, Jesus, your love is enough for me.*

Jesus, you are song I sing every day: *Jesus, you are the song, I sing every day, Jesus, you are the song I, sing every, you are the song I sing every day. Your love is too beautiful, your love too wonderful, you are the song I sing every day.*

I love this short song about love: *I found love, beautiful love, sweet love in Jesus. Jesus, I love the love you have for me!*

I love Him because He first loved me, *1 John 4:10, in this is love, not that we loved God, but that He loved us and sent His Son to the world to be propitiation for our sins.*

1 John 4:19, We love Him because He first loved us.

what manner of Man is Jesus, *Matthew 8:27, and the men marvelled, saying what manner of Man is this, that even the wind and the sea obey Him?*

I love Him so- much that I cannot do with Him, someone like Him, who can find? He is so sweet, have you tasted His love? *Psalms 34:8,taste and see that the Lord is good, blessed is the man who trusts in Him!*

John 3:11(b), Jesus that his hour had come that He should depart from this world to the Father, having love His own who were in the world, He loved them to the end.

Jeremiah 31:3-4, The Lord appeared of old to me saying, "Yes, I have loved you with an everlasting love: therefore with loving-kindness I have drown you. Again I will build you and you shall be rebuilt.

His love never cease, *Lamentation 3:22, the steady fast love of the Lord never ceases, His mercies never come to an end.*

Ephesians 2:4, But who is rich in mercy because of His great **love** *which He loved us.*

Ephesians 5:25, Husbands, love your wives just as Christ also loved the church, (us) and gave Himself for it, that He might sanctify and cleanse it with the washing of water by the word.

Romans 8:37, Yes, in all these we are more than conquerors through Jesus who loved us. Psalm 63:3, Because your loving-kindness is better than life, I shall praise you.

Songs of Solomon 2:4, His banner over me is love.

Zephaniah 3:17, The Lord God is in our midst, the Mighty one, will save, He will rejoice over me with gladness, He will quiet me in His love, He will rejoice over me with singing.

His love is so amazing, His love is so wonderful, sweet love and He promised never to leave me.

Deuteronomy 31:6, I, will be strong and be of good courage, I will not fear nor be afraid for the Lord goes before me, He will never leave me nor forsake me.

Romans 8:31, What then shall I say, to these things, if God be for me, who can be against me?

He is always with me and He will always be with me, as long as I am with Him, I will never be afraid of those things that raise their heads against me! Ever present God, Jehovah Shammah, every present help in time of need. I can say with all assurance that my future is in His hands. *Psalm 31,:15, says, my times are in your hand, Lord, deliver me from the hand of my enemy, and from those who persecute me.*

1John 4:18, there is no fear in love but perfect love casts out fear because fear involves torment, but he who fears has not been made perfect in love.

I love, love, why? Because love goes all the way!

1 corinthians 13:8, Love never fails (Jesus never fails.)

1corinthian 8:13, And now abide with faith, hope, love, these three but the greatest of all, is love.

1 corinthians 8:4, Love suffers long and is kind, love does not envy. Love does not parade itself, it is not puffed up.

1 Corinthians 16:14, Let all you do, be done in love.

1 corinthians 8:5-7, Love does not behave rudely, love does not seek its own, love is not provoked , love does not think evil. Love does not rejoice in iniquity but rejoices in truth, love bear all things, love believes all things, love endures all things, love hopes all things.

Romans 8:35, Who can separate us (me) from the love of God?

Romans 83:39, Nor heights, depth, nor any other created thing shall be able to separate us (me) from the love which is in Christ Jesus our Lord.

Love is beautiful, it does not pretend, I love it when love is sincere!

1 Corinthians, 13:1-3, Paul said, though I speak with tongues of men and of angels, but have no love, I have become as sounding brass or clacking cymbal. And thought I have the gift of prophecy and understand all mysteries and all knowledge, and thought I have all faith, so that I could move mountains but have no love, I am nothing. And thought I bestow all my goods to feed the poor, and thought I give my body to be burned , but have no love, it profit me nothing.

Ephesians 5:1-2, Therefore be followers of God as dear children, and walk in love as Christ also has loved us and given Himself for us, an offering and sacrifice to God for a sweet smelling aroma.

1 Corinthians 14:1, Pursue love- Pursue God.

2 Corinthians 13:14,The grace of our Lord Jesus Christ, and the love of God, and the communion of the Holy Spirit be with you all. Amen.

When I was still in Uganda we there is a song we sang, I said, those were days when I did not have wisdom to understand the power behind songs! All I did was to enjoy a good song, but now!

Stay in love my brother, stay in love. Stay in love my brother stay in love.

Love that mend a broken heart, love that gives victory, so, stay in love my brother stay in love.

Can you imagine I did not know the meaning of this song! Now, who gives us victory? And who mend a broken heart? But God.

Proverbs 21:3, The horse is prepared for the day of battle, but deliverance is of the Lord.

Isaiah 59:19, When the enemy comes in like a flood, the spirit of the Lord will lift up a standard against him.

2 Corinthians 2:14, Now thanks be to God who always lead us in triumph in Christ and through us diffuses the fragrance of His knowledge in every place.

1John 5:4-5, For whatever is born of God overcomes the world, and this is the victory that has overcomes the world- our faith. Who is he who overcomes the world, but he who believes that Jesus is the Son of God.

1 Corinthians 10:4-5, For the weapons of welfare are not carnal but mighty in God for pulling down strongholds, casting down arguments and every high thing that exalts itself against the knowledge of God, bringing every high thought into captivity to the obedience of Christ.

Psalm 3:8, Salvation belongs to the Lord, your blessing is upon your people

Psalm 20:7-8, Some trust in chariots and some in horses; but we will remember the name of the Lord our God. The have bowed down and fallen; but we have risen and stood up right.

Exodus 14:13-14, And Moses said to the people, "Do not be afraid, stand still and see the salvation of the Lord which He will accomplish for you today. For the Egyptian whom you see today, you shall see them again no more forever. The Lord will fight for you today and you shall hold your peace.

Exodus 15:1-3, "I will sing to the Lord for Hewlett has triumphed gloriously, the and its rider He has thrown into the sea! The Lord is my strength and my song, He has become my salvation. He is my God and I will praise Him: my Father's God, I will exalt Him. The Lord is a Man of war, the Lord is His name.

Exodus 15:9-10, The enemy said, "I will pursue, I will overtake, I will divide the spoil, my desire shall be satisfied on them. I will draw my sword, my hand shall destroy them. You blew with your wind, the sea covered them, they sank like lead in the mighty waters.

Exodus 15:12-13, You stretched out your right hand: the earth swallowed them, you, in your mercy you have led forth the people whom you have redeemed, you have guided them in your strength to your holy habitation.

1 Samuel 17:45-47, Then David said to the Philistine, you come to me with a sword, with a spear and with javelin, but I come to you in the name of Lord of hosts, the God of armies of Israel whom you have defiled.

V46, This day the Lord will deliver you into my hand and I will strike you and take your head off from you. And this day I will give carcasses of the camp of the Philistines to the birds of the air and the wild beasts of the earth, that all the earth may know that there is a God in Israel.

V47, Then all this assembly shall know that the Lord does not save with sword and spear, for the battle is the Lord's and He give you into our hands.

Ephesians 6:10-11, Be strong in the Lord and in the power of His mighty, put on the whole armour of God, that you may be able to stand against the wiles of the devil.

He is my shepherd, *psalm 23:1-2, The Lord is my shepherd I shall not want, He makes me to lie down in the green pasture, He leads me beside still waters.*

He takes care of my need, *Psalms 68:19, blessed be the Lord who daily loads me with benefits, the God of my salvation.*

Philippians 4:19, and my God shall supply all my needs according to His riches in glory by Jesus Christ.

This comes with a song: *Oh Lord I praise you, oh Lord I praise you, oh Lord I praise you, oh Lord, I praise you.*

Great Iam, All Sufficient God, you supply all my needs, oh Lord I praise you.

Dressed in Majesty, clothed in honour, you are full of glory, oh Lord I praise you.

Consuming fire, merciful God, you full of patience, oh Lord I praise you.

I am proud to know that He loves me, before I, met Him, I was looking and really searching for someone like Him but he was nowhere to be found! Why ? Because

I needed someone who could love me and accept me no matter what state! Someone who does not have time to judge me, because the Bible says:

John 3:17, for God did not send His son into the world to condemn the world, but that the world through Him might be saved.

I wanted Him who would polish me (my life) to make me new.

In *Matthew 8:2 says, and behold a leper came and worshipped Him, saying, "Lord, if you are willing, you can make me clean.*

Psalm 51:10, Create in me a clean heart, O God and renew a steadfast spirit within me.

I needed someone whose hands are always open, the one whose understanding is unreachable.

Isaiah 40:28, have you not known? Have you not heard? The Everlasting God, the Lord, the Creator of the end of the earth, neither faints, nor is weary, His understanding is unsearchable.

I was searching of the faithful one and trust worthy, *2 Thessalonians 3:3, the Lord is faithful, who will establish you and guard you from the evil one.*

1 Thessalonians 5 v 24, Faithful is He who calls you and He will bring it to pass.

Someone who will not allow me to be ashamed, *Romans 10:11, whoever believes on Him shall never be put to shame.*

1 Peter 2 v 6, Behold, I lay Zion A Chief corner- stone, electric, precious, and he who believes on Him will by no means be put to shame.

I wanted someone so great and so kind, whose words can never fall to the ground, once He speaks, you know that He has spoken, no corners, that Man, who knows how to respects His words and stand by what He says. a Man whose words I'm able to count on, when he says a word I know it is true,

Isaiah 40:8, says the grass withers, the flower fades but the word of God stands forever.

Matthew 24:35, Heaven and earth will pass away but my words will by no means pass away.

Jeremiah 1:12, Then the Lord said to me, "you have seen well, for I am ready to perform my word."

Isaiah 55:11, So shall my words be that goes forth from my mouth; it shall not return to me Void but it shall accomplish what I please, and it shall prosper in the thing for which I sent it.

When He says yes it is yes, when He says no, it is no! I mean someone whose words and character are not twisted. The impossible doer and never a liar and a deceiver,

Psalms 89:35, Once I have sworn by my holiness, I will not lie to David.

Numbers 23:19, God is not a man that He should lie, nor the son of man that He should repent. Has He said, it shall come to pass.

Someone who's word is sweet, *psalms 119:103, says, how sweet are your word to my taste, sweeter than honey to my mouth!*

I wanted someone whom I follow and never be lost, one who will never disappoint me. The one I can call reliable and dependable, the comforter.

Expert in mending a broken heart, *psalms 34 :18, tells me that the Lord is close to the broken hearted.*

Psalm 147:3, He heals the broken heart and binds up their wounds.

I needed the Prince of peace, Shalom, *John 14:27*[A] *He says, my peace I leave with you, my peace I give to you, not as the world gives do I give to you.*

Psalm 4:7-8, You have put gladness in my heart, more than the season that their grain increased. I will both lie down in peace, and sleep for you a lone O Lord, make me dwell in peace.

One able to calm the storm in my boat;

Mark 4:37–39, And the great storm arose and the wave beat into the boat so that it was already filling, but Jesus was in the stern asleep on the pillow, and they woke Him and said to Him, "Teacher, do you not care that we are perishing?" Then He arose and rebuked the wind and said to the sea, "peace be still, and the wind ceased and there was great calm.

John 16:33, These things I have spoken to you, that in me you may have peace, in the world you will have tribulations, but be of good cheer, I have over come the world.

Philippians 4:7, And the peace of God which surpasses all understanding will guard my heart and my mind through Christ Jesus. (Even in this time of trouble (pandemic) He shall fill my heart with peace!

Someone faithful and true.

Revelation 19:11, Then I saw heaven opened and behold a white horse and He who sat on was called faithful and true and in righteousness He judges and make wars.

Psalm 92:2, To declare your loving-kindness in the morning and your faithfulness every night.

Revelation 3:14, the Amen, the faithful and true witness, the beginning of God's creation of God.

1 Corinthians 1:9, God is faithful by Him I, was called into the fellowship with His son Jesus Christ my Lord.

Psalm 89:8, O, Lord God of hosts, who is like you, Lord? Your faithfulness also surrounds you.

Someone I could talk to and talk about all the time, the one who's words I can stand on: *psalm 119:105, says, your word is a lamp to my feet and my path.*

Psalm 1:1, But his delight is in the law of the Lord and His law he meditate day and night.

Psalm 89:34,"My covenant I will not violate nor will alter the utterance of lips.

Psalm 110:4, The Lord has sworn and will not change His mind, "You are a priest forever, in the order of Melchizedek."(niv)

Psalm 119:50, This is my comfort in affliction, for your word has given me life. Psalm 119:140, Your word is pure, therefore your servant loves it.

Psalm 119:162, I rejoice in your word as one who finds great treasures.

Psalm 119: 173, My tongue shall speak of your word, for all your commandments are righteous.

Psalm 119: 172, My lips shall utter praise for you teach me your statutes.

Psalm 119:114, You are my hiding place and my shield, I hope in your word.

Psalm 119 :116, Uphold me according to your word that I may live.

Psalm 119 :147, I rise before the dawning of the morning, and cry for help, I hope in your word.

Psalm 119:89, Forever, O Lord your word is settled in heaven. 2 corinthians 1:20, For all the promises of God in Him are yes and in Him are Amen to the glory of God through us.

In fact I wanted that Man whose name is Word. *Revelation 19: 12-13, His eyes were like a flame of fire, and on His head were many crowns, He had a name written that no one knew except Himself. He was clothed with a robe dipped in the blood, and His name is called Word of God.*

John 1:1,In the beginning was the Word, and the Word was with God, and the Word was God.

John 1:14, And the word became fresh and dwelt among us and we beheld His glory, the glory as the only begotten of the Father, full of grace and truth.

Someone who can hold me firm, *Psalms 62:2, He is my only Rock and my salvation, He is my defence, I shall not be moved.*

Psalms 18:46, the Lord lives, blessed be my Rock, let the God of salvation be exalted.

Psalm 95:1, let us shout joyfully to the Rock of our salvation.

Psalm 27:5, For in the time of trouble He shall hide me in His pavilion, in the secret place of His tabernacle He shall hide. He shall set me high upon a rock.

I wanted a refuge.

in time of trouble, *Psalm 46: 1, God is my refuge and strength, a very present help in times of trouble.*

I will say of the Lord, He is my refuge and my fortress, my God in Him I will trust, ***psalm 91:2***

Someone who can hid me from pestilence and covers me, here is one of my favourite psalms;

psalm 91:1, He who dwells in the secret place of the Most High, shall abide under the shadow of the Almighty. v2, I will say of the Lord," He is my Refuge and my fortress, my God in Him I will trust.

v3, Surely He shall deliver me from the snare of the fowler and from the deadly pestilence.

V4, He shall cover me with His feathers, and under His wings I shall take refuge, His truth shall be my shield buckler.

v5, I shall not be afraid of the terror by night, nor the arrow that flies by day,

v6, nor of the pestilence that walks in the darkness, nor the destruction that lays waste at noon day.

V7, A thousand may fall at my side, and ten thousand at my right hand but it shall not come near me. v8, only with my eyes shall I, look and see the punishment of the wicked.

v9, because I have made the Lord who is my refuge, even the Most High my dwelling place.

v10, No evil shall befall me, nor shall any plaque come near my dwelling.

v11, for He shall give His angels charge over me to keep me in all my ways.

v12, In their hands, they shall bear me up, lest I dash my foot against a stone.

V13, I shall tread upon the lion and the cobra, the young lion and the serpent I, shall trample underfoot.

v14, Because I have set my love upon Him, therefore He will deliver me, He will set me on high because I have known His Name.

v15, I shall call upon Him, and He will answer me, He will be with me in trouble, He will deliver me and honour me. v16, with long life He will satisfy me, and show me His salvation." Hallelujah!

I needed someone who is able to restore,

Jeremiah 30:17, But I will restore you to health and heal your wound, declares the Lord," because you are called you an outcast saying this is Zion no one seeks her, (for whom no one cares.)

Joel 2:25, I will restore to you the years that the swarming locust has eaten, the crawling locust and the consuming locust, and chewing locust, my great army which I sent among you.

Psalm 51:12, Restore to me the joy your salvation and uphold me by your generous spirit.

Psalm 23:3, He restores my soul, He guide me in the path of righteousness for His name's sake.

Someone who thinks good thoughts *towards me:*

Jeremiah 29:11, for I know the thoughts I think towards you, says the Lord, thoughts of peace and not of evil, to give you a future and a hope.

Someone in whom I have my being;

Acts 17: 28, in Him I live and move and have my being.

Colossians, 1:27,Christ in me the hope of glory.

Job 33:4, The spirit of God has made me and the breath of the Almighty gives me life. Colossians 2:10, and I'm complete in Him, who is the head of all principalities and power.

1John 4:4, I'm God's child and I have overcome them, because Greater is He that is in me than he who is in the world.

Psalm 36:9, for with Him is the is fountain of life, in His light I see light.

Job 12:10, In whose hand is the life of every living thing, and the breath of every mankind.

Someone able to make a new.

Isaiah 43:18-19, do not remember the former things, nor consider the things of old. Behold I do a new thing, now it shall spring forth, shall you not know it? I will even make road in the wilderness and rivers in the desert.

The one who tells me, do not fear I'm with you:

Joshua 1:9, Have I not commanded you? Be stronger and of good courage, do not be afraid, nor be dismayed, for the Lord your God is with you wherever you go."

Luke 2:30, And the angle said me, do not be afraid, for you have found favour with God.

Luke 2:13, But the angle said to me, do not be afraid, for prayer is heard.

Psalms 127:1, The Lord is my light and my salvation, whom shall I fear? The Lord is the strength of my life, of whom shall I be afraid?

Isaiah 40:10, The Lord says to me, t for I'm with you; be not dismayed for I'm your God, I will strengthen you, yes, I will help you, I will uphold you with my righteous right hand.

Psalms 23:4, Yea, though I walk through the valley of the shadow of death, I will fear not evil, for you are with me, your rod and your staff, the comfort me.

Isaiah 10:14, I hear a voice says, fear not, I will help you," says the Lord, and your Redeemer, the Holy one of Israel.

Isaiah 10:13, He tells me, for I, the Lord your God will hold your right hand saying to you, "Fear not, I will help you.

One who is able fight for me, *Joshua 1:5, He says to me, no man shall be able to stand before me, as He was with Moses so He will be with me.*

Deuteronomy 20:4, for the Lord my God is He who goes with me to fight for **me** against **my** enemies to save me.

Deuteronomy 3:22, ***I will*** *not fear them, for the Lord* ***my*** *God Himself fights for me.*

Psalms 118:6, the Lord is on my side, I will not fear, what can man do to me?

One who has power to bless me and no man can stand to start curse! Because I have seen that some people like to give themselves power to curse as if they have what it takes to curse others! One time someone asked me, Betty, do you want me to curse you? Do you want me to ask God you kill you? I answered, you can never have power to curse me and if you try it will only return back to you!

Numbers 6:24-26, *The Lord will bless me and keep me, the Lord make His face shine upon me. And the Lord be gracious to me. The Lord lifts up His countenance upon me and give me peace.*

Blessed shall I, be when I come in, and blessed shall I be when I go out, Deuteronomy 28:6.

Deuteronomy 28:5, Blessed shall be my basket and my kneading bowl.

Deuteronomy 28:3, Blessed shall I, be in the city and blessed shall I be in the country.

Deuteronomy 28:12, The Lord will open to me His good treasure, the heaven to give the rain to my land in its season, and bless all the work of my hands. I shall lend to many nations, but I shall not borrow.

And the Lord will make me the head and not the tail, I shall be above only and not beneath, Deuteronomy 28:13.

My gates shall be open continually they shall not be shut day or night that men may bring me wealth of the Gentile and their kings in possession, Isaiah 60:11.

Who is able to make me sing new song, turn my mourning to dancing, turn misery into ministry, set my feet upon the rock and to give me double honour for my shame.

He has put a new song in my mouth, praise to our God, many will see it and fear and will trust in the Lord, psalm 40:3.

He has brought me up out of a horrible pit, out of Miry clay and set my feet upon rock, psalm 40:2.

Lord by your favour you have made my mountain stand strong, psalm 30:7.

You turned my mourning into dancing, you have put off my sackcloth and clothed me with gladness, psalm 30:11.

He is my hiding place, He shall preserve me from trouble and surround me with songs of deliverance, psalm 32:7.

The Lord will command His loving kindness in the daytime and in the night His songs shall be with me, psalm 42:8.

Psalm 43:5, Why are cast down, or my soul? And why are you disquieted within me? Hope in God for I will yet praise Him, the help of my countenance and my God,

He is able to give me beauty for ashes, the oil of joy for mourning, the garment of praise for the spirit of heaviness, Isaiah 61:3.

SHINE, Isaiah 60:1–2, I will arise and shine for my light has come and the glory of the Lord is risen upon me.

For behold the darkness shall cover the earth but the deep darkness the people but Lord will arise over me and His glory will be seen upon me.

Isaiah 60:3, the Gentiles shall come to my light and Kings to the brightness of my rising.

Isaiah 60:5, I shall see and become radiant, my heart shall swell with joy because the abundance of the sea shall be turned to me and the wealth of the Gentiles shall come to me.

Matthew 5:14, you are the light in this world, a city that is set on the hill which cannot be hidden.

Matthew 5:16, So let your light so shine before men that they may see the good works and glorify your Father in heaven.

- Psalms 36:9, For with you is the fountain of life, in your light I, see light.

I wanted Him who is able to teach me, a Teacher!

Psalm 90:12, So teach us to number our days that we my gain a heart of wisdom.

Psalm 71:17, O God, you have taught me from my youth, and to this day I declare your wondrous works.

Psalm 25:8, Good and upright is the Lord, therefore He teaches sinners in the way.

Job 35:11, Who teaches us more than the beasts of earth, and makes us wiser than the birds of heaven.

Job 22:22, Receive instructions from His word, and lay up His word in your heart.

Job 34:32, Teach me what I do not see, if I have done iniquity, I will do no more!"

Psalm 32:8, I will instruct you in the way you should go, I will guide you with my eye.

Psalm 86:11, Teach me your way O Lord, I will walk in your truth, unite my heart you fear your name.

Proverbs 22:6, Train up a child in the way he should go, and when he is old he will not depart from it.

Proverbs 9:9, Give instructions to a wise man and he will be still wise, teach a just man, and he will increase in learning.

Isaiah 48:17, Thus says the Lord, your Redeemer the Holy one of Israel, I'm the Lord your God who teaches you to profit. Who leads you by the way you should go.

Isaiah 54:13, All young children shall be taught by the Lord, and great shall be the peace of your children.

Exodus 4:12, Now therefore, go and I will be with your mouth and teach you what you shall say.

Psalm 119:99, I have more understanding than all my teachers, for your testimonies are my meditation.

Exodus 4:15, Now, you shall speak to him and put the words in his mouth, and I will be with your mouth and his mouth, and I will teach you what you should do.

Luke 4:15, And He taught in their Synagogues being glorified by all.

Luke 5:3, And Jesus got into one of the boats which was Simon's and asked him to put out a little from the land, and He sat down and taught and the multitudes from the boat.

John 3:2,This man came to Jesus at night and said to Him, "Rabbi, we know that you are a teacher comes from God: for no one can do these signs unless God is with Him.!"

John 8:2, But early in the morning Jesus came again into the temple, and all the people came to Him and He sat down and taught them.

John 7:14-15, Now about the middle of the feast, Jesus went up into the temple and taught. And the Jews marvelled, saying, how does this Man know letters , never have studied?"

Psalm 143:10, Teach me to do your will, for you are my God, your spirit is good, lead me in the land of up rightness.

What about wisdom! One is able to show me how to be wise!

Proverbs 9:10, The fear of the Lord is the beginning of wisdom, and the knowledge of the Holy one is understanding.

Joshua 1:8, This book of the law shall not depart from your mouth, but you shall meditate on it day and night that you may observe to do according to all that is written in it for then you will make your way prosperous and then you will have good success.

Proverbs 2:10, When wisdom enters your heart, and is pleasant you your soul.

Psalm 51:6, Behold you desire truth in the inward parts, and in the hidden parts you will make me to know wisdom.

Isaiah 28:29, This also comes from the Lord of hosts who is wonderful in counsel and excellent in guidance.

Daniel 2:20, Daniel answered and said, blessed be the name of God forever, for wisdom and might are His,

Daniel 1:17, As for these four young men, God gave them knowledge and skills in all literature and wisdom: and Daniel had understanding in all visions and dreams.

Job 28:12-13, But where can wisdom be found? And where is the place of understanding? Man does not know it's value nor is it found in the land of the living.

Luke 2:40, And the child grew and became strong in spirit, filled with wisdom and the grace of God was upon Him.

Ecclesiastes 9:16, Wisdom is better than strength, nevertheless the poor man's wisdom is despised and his words are not heard.

Ecclesiastes 9:18, Wisdom is better than weapons of war, but one sinner destroys much good.

James 1:5, If anyone lack wisdom let him ask of God, who give to all liberally and without reproach and it will be given to him.

Job 28: For the price of wisdom is far above rubies.

Daniel 12:3, Those who are wise shall shine like the brightness of the firmament and who turn many to righteousness like the stars for ever and even.

Luke 21:15, For I will give you a mouth and wisdom which all your adversaries will not be able to contradict or resist.

Job 28:20-21, From where then does wisdom come? And where is the place of understanding? It is hidden from the eyes of all living and concealed from the birds of the air.

Romans 11:33, Oh, the depth of the riches both of wisdom and knowledge of God! How unreachable are His judgement and His ways pass finding out.

Job 12:22, He uncovers deep things out of the darkness, and brings shadow of death to light.

Proverbs 8:1- ,Does not wisdom cry out and understanding lift up her voice? She take her stand on the top of the high hill, beside the where the path meet she cries out by the gate, at the entrance of the doors, "To you o men I call and my is to the sons of men. Oh you simple ones and you fools, be of understanding heart.

Job 12:13, With Him are wisdom and strength, He has counsel and understanding.

Proverbs 8:34-36, Blessed is the man who listens to me, watching daily at my gate, waiting at the posts of my doors. Whoever finds me, find life, and obtains favour from the Lord. But he who sins against me wrongs his own soul.

Proverbs 8:17-19, I love them who love me and those who seek me diligently shall find me. Riches and honour are with me, enduring riches and righteousness, my fruit is better than gold, yes than fine gold, and my revenue that choice sliver.

Job 28:27-28, Then He saw wisdom and declared it, He prepared it, indeed he searched it out, And to a man He said, behold the fear of the Lord, that is wisdom, and to depart from evil, is understanding.

2 Chronicles 2:10, Now give me wisdom and knowledge that I may go out and come in before these people, for can judge this great people of yours?"

2 Chronicles 2:12, Wisdom and Knowledge are granted to you, and I will give you riches and wealth and honour, such as none of the Kings have had who have been before you, nor shall any after you have the like.

2 Chronicles 9:2-3, So Solomon answered all her questions, there was nothing difficult for Solomon that he could not explain to her. And when the Queen of Sheba had had seen the wisdom of Solomon, the house that he had built........!

2 Chronicles 9:6-7, The Queen of Sheba said to Solomon, however, I did not believe their words until I came and saw with my own eyes, and the half of the greatness of your wisdom was not told me. You exceed the fame of which I heard. Happy are your men and happy are these your servant, who stand continually before you and hear your wisdom.

Exodus 31:1-5, Then God spoke to Moses, saying," see I have called by name Bezaleel, the son of uri, of the tribe Judah. And I have filled him with the Spirit of God in wisdom, understanding, in knowledge, and in all manners of workmanship. To design artistic work, to work in gold, in sliver, in bronze, in cutting jewels for setting, curving wood and to work in all manners of workmanship.

Colossians 2:2-3, That their hearts may be encouraged being knit together in love and attaining to all riches of the full assurance of understanding to the knowledge of the mystery of God, both of the Father and of Christ. In who are hidden all the treasures of wisdom and knowledge.

1Kings 3:12(a), And said to Solomon, behold, I have done according to your word, see, I have given you a wise and understanding heart.

1Kings 4:29-31, And God gave Solomon wisdom and exceedingly great understanding, and largeness of heart like the sand on the sea-shore. Thus Solomon's wisdom excelled the wisdom of all men of the earth and all the wisdom of Egypt. For he was wiser than all men...and his fame was in all surrounding nations. Solomon spoke three thousand proverbs and his songs were a thousand and five. Also he spoke of the trees from cedar tree of Lebanon even to the hyssop that springs out of the wall: he spoke also of animals, of birds, of creeping things and of fish. Men of all nations, from the king's of the earth who heard of his wisdom, came to hear the wisdom of Solomon.

I am so happy I found Him, beautiful love- Jesus, It's Him, I have to shout it loud, I love Jesus, I love the way He cares about me, sweet caring darling Jesus. I cannot spend a day without talking to Him, I love being with Him and I love to talking to Him because when you love someone, you want to be with that person all the time. I love talking about Him, *this is not gossiping!* He is so different He can never ignore a phone call or put His phone in voice mail! In fact He says to me, call me and I will answer;

Jeremiah 33:3, call me and I will answer you, and show you great and might things which you do not know.

I wrote a song that says when I call on Him, He answers:

My Redeemer, my Redeemer, my Redeemer, oh
I will give you all the glory, I will give you all the glory
My Redeemer, my Redeemer, my Redeemer, oh
I will give you all the glory, I will give you all the glory
Jesus, Jesus, Jesus, I will give you all the glory

Jesus, Jesus, Jesus, I will give you all the glory
When I call on you, you really answer me
When I call you, you really answer me,
When I call on you, Jesus, you really answer me,
oh I will give you all the glory.
What you do, no man can do, what you do, no man can do
What you do no man can do, I will give you all the glory.
My Redeemer, my Redeemer, my Redeemer, oh
I will give you all the glory, I will give you all the glory.

These the kind of songs I sang when I had nothing else to do but to worship. And I knew that through my praise I was talking to God about some issues, those issues that had brought restrictions on me and caused me not to leave a free life at that time. Because no **paper, no freedom!** *But I had my freedom to worship!* In fact when I look back, I thank God for that time because it gave me a chance to get close to God. I did not want to spend a time without Him, my precious love. My songs became that love letter or love noise in His eye.

Spending some time without seeing someone you love, you automatically know that something is missing. If there is a friend I never want to miss out on, is Jesus! I can't help it because when you love someone, you can be crazy in a good way! It's a beautiful thing to talk about Jesus- my beautiful love, He knows how I feel about Him. I used to hear those advisers of mine (wicked women) those who were advising me with evil minds but tried to cover with good words. I heard someone say, Betty, I have got someone for you! Heeh, Someone to keep you company, you need someone who will give you visa, give you a house. You must learn to use these men, then as soon as you get what you want, you leave them. What a wicked advice! I used to wonder at such advice, you may think that you are using him to get settled but what you forget is, you are using yourself and selling yourself very cheap just get what you will eat the following day! These, women, they speak with that sweet tongue but underneath is poison in the cup! Their plan was to see me fall! So if that is the case, that some women use men to get food for the next day, why not hook up with Jesus at least He already bought me with a high price. He paid it all for me with His blood, I belong to Him and Him alone.

1 Corinthians 6:20, For you were bought at price, therefore glorify God in your body and in your spirit which are God's.

1 Corinthians 7:23, You are bought at a price, do not become slaves to men.

No man will use me, for theirs is misery, I mean those! I have arms to work, I will not you Mr man survive. Let Jesus use me and use me for His glory, He will use me and give me eternal life. He will take care of me here and still grant me life without end. Because if you put your heart on serving Jesus, your treasure will be in Jesus. And if you put your heart in earthly men, then your treasure will be on earthly men. And remember you will never be satisfied, you will continue to hunger because you will be looking for who to use next. Let Jesus use you He is enough, Jesus will never look for who to use and throw away when no longer needed! In fact He knows how to beautify His own. He gave me this song and whenever I sing it I feel Him with me, you are the one I love:

You are the one I love, You are the one
You the one I talked about all the time,
Jesus Almighty God is your name, you are the one
I talk about all the time, Jesus.
Almighty God, is your name,
Your the one I, talk about all the time, Jesus.

There is something about Jesus, I feel happy being with Him, I feel happy talking to Him and it makes me very happy when I talk about Him. I can't really explain the love of Jesus, It's unexplainable! Who can talk about Jesus' love and finish? I want Him like never before! What else can I do If I don't sing?

Daddy, Daddy, Daddy Jesus, I want you like never before,
I'm in love you Jesus, I want you like never before.
I cannot do without you- Jesus, I want you like never before.
To worship you Jesus, I want you like never before.
To do your work Jesus, I want like never before.

A man called Jesus truly is a Man of love, *He who was blind answered,*

John 9 :11, A man called Jesus made clay and anointed my eyes and said to me, go and wash to the pool of Siloam and wash, so I went and washed and received sight,

A man called Jesus is a man of love,
A Man called Jesus is a Man of love.
He loves me, He loves me,
He loves me, He loves me.
A man called Jesus is a man of love!
Oh Jesus you love me, I know, I know, I know you love me Father,
Oh Jesus, you love me, I know, I know you care about me.
Oh Jesus, I will praise you, oh Jesus, I will honour you Father,
Oh Jesus, I will adore you, because I know you care about me,
What a wonderful Father, you are to me, what a wonderful
Father, What a wonderful Father, what a wonderful God.
I love you, Jesus, I love you, I love you, you are a wonderful God.
I thank you, Jesus, I thank you, I thank you, you are a wonderful God.
I praise you, Jesus, I praise you, I praise you, you are a wonderful God.

In Uganda we used to sing this song but in those days I did not catch the meaning so I just enjoyed the song. But when I came to understand it, is really loaded! Song:

Your love Jesus I can't understand,
your love Jesus I can't understand,
Your love Jesus, I can't understand.
Your love that made to leave your father,
your love that made you to be a lonely man,
your love that made you to die on the cross,
your love Jesus, I can't understand!

Jesus' love towards us is endless, He is rich in love, His love is a river which never runs dry. Everything about Jesus is sweet, I would love to give Him something to show how much I love Him, I would love to show Him how much I appreciate Him, but what can I give to someone who owes the whole universe, He owes heaven and earth. What can I give to someone so-big? He fills the heaven the earth is His footstool! Oh my God, how big are you! You are as big as I make you to be! If I was to build a house for you I would choose the best of the best design but then, you don't live in houses built by men.

Isaiah 66:1 says *heaven is my throne, earth is my footstool, where is the house you will build for me and where is the place of my rest?*

He owes a thousand cattle on a hills, *Psalms 50:10-12, for every beast of the forest is mine, and the cattle on a thousand hills. I know all the birds of the mountains, and the wild beasts of the field are mine. If I were hungry, I would not tell you, for the world is mine and all it's fullness*

Someone may ask, why do you love Jesus? I think the easiest answer would be, I love Him because He is mine, I love Him because He came all the way from heaven Just to give me life and of course He is my God. Thank you Jesus for all you have done, for what you are doing and for you are yet to do. My mother used to tell us that we all have two types friends, a friend who loves you and a friend you love! According to my mother, the sold friend is a friend that loves you, because a friend you love, also loves someone but this is not in Jesus' case. My son puts it this way, Jesus loves me fully, He loves me fully! While struggling to answer how much Jesus love him! There many reasons to love Jesus, so I can say, I love Him because of who His to me, He is my everything, my all in all. It was love that made Him to do what He did, love made Him to die on the cross, all my sins, my shame and guilty were nailed with Him to the cross at Calvary. Jesus carried that heavy cross just for me, it was not easy at all. My elven years old son was preaching to me in the house, he was preaching to a big congregation and said, no wonder Jesus fell many times carrying that big cross! It was heavy, my son continued his message, all our sins were in that cross, sins that people had committed and sins that we were going to commit were all in that big fat cross! I said what? ***John 19:17-18, And He bearing His cross went out to a place of a skull, which is called Golgotha. Where they crucified Him and two others with Him, one either side and Jesus the middle***. He shed His blood for me, sweet blood to my tongue, precious blood of Jesus shed for me. I call it acidic, poisonous blood to the kingdom of darkness. There is power, might power in the blood Jesus. I drink the blood of Jesus every morning, I put hands on my mouth as if I'm drinking something and then say, I drink the blood of Jesus, I give it to my son, I call every person's name that comes on my mouth and say, drink the blood of Jesus, I know it is sweet to me but I use it as weapon because evil cannot stand it! I don't know how it all started that I should drink the blood of Jesus but it has worked. It is cleanses the system and removes every junk. I noticed that after I had started drinking the blood of Jesus strange things started to happen. I found out that in my dreams I throw up (vomit) it looks real in my sleep as if I'm standing beside the sink. It was funny that one night in my dreams I actually pulled a rubbish bin after throwing up my stomach was empty, but then I heard this woman's voice back home in my **village** as I threw up, she said, the bottle is full, no space in the bottle, she said, everything is coming out! Whatever it meant! It has become a habit, I can never eat anything, or drink any thing without covering it with the blood of Jesus. If I go out and do shopping as soon I come home I must make sure I sanctify every food/ things. I don't joke with the blood of Jesus, it's a weapon on its own. In 2018, in my sleep, I had a strange dream where I was drinking Jesus' blood, my mouth was too sweet that in the morning I did not feel like blushing my mouth. Though I cleaned my mouth I spent that day with a sweet mouth. I can't speak about Jesus' blood and finish, the Lamb who was slain, I give you glory. With your blood I over come. *Revelation 12:11, and they overcame him by the blood of the Lamb and by the words of their testimony, and they loved their lives unto death.*

Who did they overcome? That spent of old called the devil.

Revelation 12:9, so the great dragon was cast out, that serpent of old called the devil and satan who deceives the whole world, he was cast out to the earth and his angles were cast out with him.

Why should I not love Jesus? I appreciate Him with all my heart. I may not give Him silver or gold to show how much I love Him but is there something I can give Him. I may not cook for Him a delicious meal or get a glass of wine but there is something I can offer Him, and that is my worship. Sweet Jesus, I will worship you my Lord. My Jesus is not a fake-small god, small gods demand meat to fill their stomachs before they could give fake blessings. Fake small gods give fake blessings. My father and my God only you, you are true God, original God you are so real, this is what I will give to you, glory, honour, adoration and thanksgiving. I will praise you Jesus. David the psalmist *said*, in ***psalms 138:1, "I will praise you with all my heart before gods, I will sing praise to you.***

Psalms 136:2, oh give thanks to the God of gods, His Mercy endures forever. Him alone does great things. What can I give to God for being God? I will worship you my Precious Jesus! You created me to worship you, I love you my Redeemer. My worship song to you:

I love you my Redeemer, I love you my Jesus, be blessed forever, be blessed forever,
My Redeemer, my Jesus, be blessed forever more.
I love you hope, I love you my Jesus, be blessed forever, be blessed forever,
My hope, my Jesus, be blessed forever more.
I love you my healer, I love my Jesus, be blessed forever, be blessed forever,
My healer, my Jesus, be blessed forever more.
I love you peace, I love you my Jesus, be blessed forever, be blessed forever,
My peace, my Jesus, be blessed forever more.
I love you my Shelter, I love you my Jesus, be blessed forever, be blessed forever,
My Shelter, my Jesus, be blessed forever more.

I will tell those small gods that Him alone is God and worthy of my praises. I once wrote a song which says:

"I love to worship you, Jesus, I love to worship you,
I cannot do without it, I love to worship you,
I cannot help it, I love to worship you.
Consuming fire, I love to worship,
I cannot do without it, I love to worship you,
I cannot help it, I love to worship you.
Glory in the midst of fire, I love to worship,
I cannot do without it, I love to worship you,
I cannot help it, I love to worship you.

OK, I may not know how to worship but I can give Him my best. God knows that my desire is to praise Him so He gave me songs to glorify Him. All I asked was, God teach me how worship but I got more that what I wanted. I think He could have said, since you have asked me to teach you how to worship me, I will also teach you how to write songs to glorify me! God, Jehovah over giver! More than enough, you will not share your glory with anyone. Without you God I know I'm completely nothing, I appreciate you I cannot thank you enough. No wonder you gave me a song like this,

I give you my heart Jesus, make it your Kingdom
And reign, reign Jesus, my heart is your Kingdom!

To me this is a scary song, because recently I was talking to my ten years old son and said, I really need to live by what I'm writing, how can I, write what I don't resemble! So I said, God I ask that you give me grace to keep this heart clean because on this matter I can't depend on myself. If I say I will do it on my own, it will also big lie, not when I'm still in this world, my help comes from you.

Heavenly Father Jesus, I magnify you, I exalt you, I will tell every nation about your power. I will tell everyone nation about your works, you are Awesome God. You are more than what we call you, that is why you give more than what we ask for. Jesus you do what you're, you're beautiful so you do beautiful things. What a beautiful God I serve! You are one who brings beauty out of dust, ***Isaiah 61:3, to console those who mourn in zone, to give them beauty for ashes, the oil of joy for mourning.*** "You are the one who makes away in the wilderness, way maker. You make rivers to run in the desert, ***Isaiah 43:19, behold I will do a new thing, now it shall spring forth, shall you not know it? I will even make rivers in the desert.*** *Isaiah 43:16, thus says Lord, who makes a way in the sea and a path through the mighty waters.*

In my life who can be like you Jesus, I just can't but praise you, I wrote this song, who can be like you!

In my life, in my life, who can be like you Jesus?
In my life, in my life, who can be like you?
Who can be compared to you? In my life Jesus?
Who can be compared to you, in my life Jesus?
Who can be equal with you? In my life Jesus?
Who can be equal with you in my life Jesus?

You are too wonderful, in my life Jesus,
You are too amazing, I'm life Jesus.
You are too beautiful, in my life Jesus,
Rose of Sharoni, Lion of Judah, Lilly of the Valley,
Who can be equal with you?
You are too Big to lie, you are too Big to fail.
Who can be like you?

Leaving in a shared accommodation, I was once called noise a maker. All I did was to praise God, if I made noise then it was beautiful in His ear. It was better than complaining. It was because of that much love, let me lean on you Jesus because I, have found true love in you. Jesus you know how to love. in 2012 when my job was only to sing worship, I mean at the time when I did not have this ***visa!*** I wrote a song, how I love you:

How I love you, my Redeemer! how I love you my Redeemer!
how I love you, my Redeemer! I love to give you, all the glory.
How I love you, my Redeemer! how I love you, my Redeemer!
how I love you, my Redeemer! I love to give you, all the praises.
How I love you, my Redeemer! how I love you, my Redeemer,
how I love you, my Redeemer! I love to give you, all the honour.
How I love you, my Redeemer, how I love you, my Redeemer!
how I love you, my Redeemer! I love to give you, all my worship.

As some people have other gods out there and they also have reason, why they love them and call them gods, I also told my God- Jesus why I, love Him.

That is why I love you Jesus, that is why I love you,
That is why I love you Jesus, that is why I love you,
I'm serving a God never fails, a God that never fails,
A God that never fails, hallelujah, a God that never fails.
That is why I love you Jesus, that is why I love you.
That is why I love Jesus, that is why I love you.
That is why I love you, that is why I love you.
I'm serving a God that never lies, a God that never lies.

A God that never lies, hallelujah, a God that never lies.
That is why I love you, that is why I love you.
That is I love you Jesus, that is why I love you.
I'm serving a God that never changes, a changes,
A God that never changes, hallelujah, a God that never changes.
That is why I love you Jesus, that is I love you.
That is why I love you, that is why I love you.
I'm serving a God that never loses, a God that never loses,
A God that never loses, hallelujah, a God that never loses.
That is why I love you Jesus, that is why I love you.
That is why I love you Jesus, that is why I love you.
I'm serving a God that never forgets, a God that never forgets,
A God that never forgets, hallelujah, a God that never forgets.

When you love someone, you don't have to be secretive about it, Jesus publicly declared His love towards me on that day, when He died at Calvary.

Romans 5:8, But God demonstrated His own love towards us, in that while we were still sinners, Christ died for us.

So, I also need to openly love Him, my Creator, my saviour, I love you Jesus is a song:

My Creator, my Saviour, I love you Jesus, I love you.
My Creator, my Saviour, I love you Jesus, I love you.
My love for you is forever more, My love for you is forever more,
My love for you is forever more, I love you Jesus, I love you.
My love for you is not a secret, my love for you is not a secret,
My love for you is not a secret, I love you Jesus, I love you Jesus,
I announce my love Jesus, I announce my love for you,
I announce my love for you Jesus, I love you, Jesus, I love you.
Because of who you are, I love you, Because of who you are, I love you,
Because of who you are, I love you, I love you Jesus, I love you Jesus.

In that charity accommodation at that time, I looked at those women around me, especially when we went to our mother's meetings I knew that every woman there once had heard this word, *I love you!* Then later every woman was left with either pregnancy or left a lone with a child! What happened? Love vanished just like that! No wonder Jesus' love is not this type! I love talking to Jesus, The moment I start to sing worship Him, a conversation begins, especially when it's only and Him alone. My habit is, when I'm in my house in that quiet time of worship before I start singing, I invite Jesus and ask angels to sing with me. I have made some songs just to well come Jesus:"

Take Your seat Jesus:

Take your seat Jesus, take your seat,
let me worship you, let every hand clap,
let everyone hand clap, Jesus is around,
let every knee bow, let every knee bow,
let every knee bow Jesus is around.
Let every tongue sing, let every tongue,
let every tongue sing, Jesus is around.
Take your seat Jesus, take your seat Jesus,
take your seat Jesus, let me worship you.

In my home take the most beautiful place

-In my home, in my home Jesus, take the most beautiful place,
In my living room Jesus, take the most beautiful place,
In my bedroom Jesus, take the most beautiful place,
In child's bedroom, take the most beautiful place,
On my dining table Jesus, eat the most delicious food,
In my home, in my home take the most beautiful place,
In this home, in this home, take the most beautiful place.

A songs to greet Him,

I greet you Jesus, I greet you Father, I say Jesus, I love you
I greet you Father, I greet you Father, I say Jesus, I love you.
Good morning, good morning, good morning King of kings,
Good morning, good morning, good morning Lord of lords.

I praise you early in the morning:

IAM WHO IAM, I thank you early in the morning,
Jesus, I AM WHO I AM, I thank you early in the morning
King of Kings, I AM WHO I AM, I thank you early in the morning
In the morning, I thank you.
I AM WHO I AM I praise you early in the morning,
Jesus, I AM WHO I AM, I praise you early in the morning
King of kings, I AM WHO IAM, I praise you early in the morning
In the morning, I praise you.
IAM WHO IAM, I bless you early in the morning,
Jesus, IAM WHO IAM, I bless you early in the morning
King of kings, I AM WHO I AM, I bless you early in the morning
In the morning I bless you.
IAM WHO IAM I, honour you early in the morning,
Jesus, I AM WHO I AM, honour you early in the morning
King of kings, I AM WHO I AM, I honour you early in the morning
In the morning I honour you.
I AM WHO I AM, Jesus, I AM WHO I AM,
In the morning I, honour you.

It is a beautiful day,

It is a beautiful day, it is a beautiful day,
Thank you Jesus, it is a beautiful day.
It is well with me, it is well with me,
Thank you Jesus, It is well with me.
It is well with me going out, it is well with me coming back.
It is a beautiful day, thank you Jesus, It is a beautiful day.

When my son was three years old I gave him food, when he finished eating he sang:

"Jehovah Shammah I love you, I love you, I love you,
Jehovah Shammah, I praise you,
I praise you, I praise you, Jehovah Shammah.

But, really how can a three year old child write such song in his mouth? It was a mystery. At the end, I asked myself, did God send him to give me this song? Jesus, you are really beautiful, you are worthy. When too many challenges pushed me to sing, I was walking around and for some reason this song came into my sprit:

you are the only one Jesus, you are the only one Jesus,
you are the only one Jesus, worthy of my praise,
I will never, praise another god, I will praise another god,
Jesus, you are the only one, worthy of my praise,
Jesus, you are only one, worthy of my praise.
I will never love another god, I will never love another god,
Jesus, you are the only one worthy of my praise, Jesus,
you are only one, worthy of my praise, How can I worship another god!
how can I worship another god! How can I worship another God!
Jesus, you are the only one, worthy of my praise.
Why should I search for another god? why should I search for another god?
Why should search for another god?
Jesus, you are the only one worthy of my praise,
Jesus, you are the only one, worthy of my praise
Heavenly Father, I say thank you, you have done amazing,
you have done excellent, I offer you, my thanks giving,
I say thank you, thank you Jesus, I say thank you.
I appreciate you, I appreciate you Jesus,
I appreciate you my Father, take all the glory,
take all the honour, I cannot thank you enough,
I cannot thank you enough Jesus, I appreciate you,
I appreciate every thing you have done for me, I appreciate you.

I did not understand the song, because it did not match with the state I was in at that time, it was do bad! So why did I come up with such song? To me at some point I thought may be those songs did not mean any thing because songs which I was receiving were hard to explain. And I'm glad that though I did not understand messages or songs that were given to me. I took time to write everything down. Eight years later, I'm typing some of my message. One day I found myself singing a song like this:

"I am connected to Jesus, I am connected to Jesus,
I am connected to Jesus, I have the Same blood with Jesus.
He is the tree and I'm the blanch, He is the tree, I'm the branch.
Whatever Jesus eats, I eat, whatever you drinks,
I drink, I'm connected to Jesus,
I have the same blood with Jesus,
whatever flows in you, flows in me.
I will not wither, nothing can cut me from Jesus.
I have the same blood with Jesus.

At that moment I could not interpret the song but I noted each word down. *In John 15 :5 Jesus said, I am the vine, you are the branches, he who abides in me and I in him bears much fruits; for without me you can do nothing.* I believe this is the song that defeated this horrible virus because *Jesus is a tree and I am the* branch. Singing this song, "*nothing can take away from Jesus* opened my heart to know the love of Jesus, the more I pounded on those songs the more received. They all came with the same message, I *love* those the days when I was heart broken. I think some songs were today's medicine! You can receive a song without understanding the meaning behind but find out later! **Without you God I know, I'm nothing;** *Without you God I know I'm nothing, without you God I know I'm nothing*

Without you, Jesus, without you, without you God I know I'm nothing
I'm nothing, without you, I'm nothing, without you.
Touch my tongue and I will speak, touch my tongue and I will speak,
I'm nothing, without you, I'm nothing without you, I'm nothing without you.
Touch my eyes and I will see, touch my eyes and I will see,
I'm nothing, without you, I'm nothing without you, I'm nothing without you.
Touch my ears and I will hear, touch my ears and I will hear,
Jesus, I'm nothing, without you, I'm nothing without you, I'm nothing without you.
Hold my hands and I will stand, hold my hands and I will stand,
I'm nothing without you, I'm nothing without you, I'm nothing without you.
Touch my legs and I will walk, touch my legs and I will walk,
I'm nothing, without you, I'm nothing without you, I'm nothing without you.
Touch my back and I will be strong, touch my back and I will be strong,

I'm nothing, without you, I'm nothing without you, I'm nothing without you.
Without you God, I know, I'm nothing, I'm nothing without you.

When you raise hands and be frank to God, that without God you I'm completely nothing, without you there is nothing I can do.

One day again in 2012 out of hunger and confusion I talked to God through a song and said, Jesus, you are my everything;

Jesus, you are my everything, yeah yeah, you are my everything,
You are my everything, Jesus, you are my everything.
I will depend on you, Jesus, I will depend on you,
I will depend on you, Jesus, I will depend on you, because I know,
You are my everything, Jesus, you are my everything
I will believe in you, Jesus, I will believe in you,
I will believe in you, Jesus, I will believe you, because I know,
You are my everything thing, Jesus, you are my everything.
I will trust in you, Jesus, I will trust in you,
I will trust in you, Jesus, I will trust in you, because I know,
You are my everything, Jesus, you are my every thing.
I will rely on you, Jesus, I will rely on you,
I will rely on you, Jesus, I will rely on you, because I know,
You are my everything, Jesus, you are my everything.
I will lean on you, Jesus, I will lean on you,
I will lean on you, Jesus, I will lean you, because, I know,
You are my everything, Jesus, you are my everything.
I will hide in you, Jesus, I will hide in you,
I will hide in you, Jesus, I will hide in you, because I know,
You are my everything, Jesus, you are my everything.
I will hopefully in you, Jesus, I will hopefully in you,
I will hopefully in you, Jesus, I will hope in you, because I know,
You are my everything, Jesus, you are my everything.

Sometimes I would speak to myself saying, it's true man of this world may have let me down but Jesus, you can never fail! I will trust you and I will believe in you because you are my everything. The song came after I had been disappointed, I was expecting a voucher to buy food for my son, I had been looking through the window checking on post man but that weekend my voucher was not delivered. As I was disappointed going back upstairs I felt like saying, enough is enough only tears were in my eyes but I did not say anything, then all of a sudden I heard these words running through my head. Jesus, you are my everything when I opened my mouth, it was a song ministering to me. I sang it and wrote it. It's true my help comes from God.

psalm 121:2-3, My help comes from the Lord who made heaven and earth, He will not allow my feet to be moved.

Hebrew 12:2,looking unto Jesus, the author and the finisher of our faith, who for the joy that was set before Him endured the cross, despising the shame and had sat down at the right hand of the throne of God.

How can confusion and disappointment give birth to a song that would minister to me and give me comfort! The following Monday my voucher came, I was at peace that weekend God provided and it was even more than enough.

I can really say that I started writing this book at the time when I was in confusion, I was trying to capture the meaning of love. Though I could have interpreted wrongly because God's love is uncomfortable. I was depending on charity because the man who once said, I love you Betty, was no where to be found. He decided to ran for his life and there I was judging myself and asking myself questions if the dream I saw, that very morning when I met him, was from devil or from God! Because how can you dream about a man you had never met at all, I did not know that this man was created either! I never knew once God made a man that looks like him! But some how God or devil brought this man in my dream very early in the morning. Every thing I saw about him that morning is how he appeared to me that very day while at work! What a description! But later the wind took him. What annoyed me more is, he couldn't even call to check on the child and If tried calling him a voicemail would answer me! I was busy lying to our son, when asked, mum, where is my daddy? I want my daddy to tie my shoelaces. Mum, daddy will come and tie my shoelaces! My only words were, daddy went on a business trip, he will come! But how many years do people go for a business trip?

I'm so happy that the situation made me to find Jesus again! Yes, again! They say, you can run but you can't escape love, remembering my mother's teaching as a child, my mother would seat us in a circle after dinner, I can still see those nights as we roasted sweet corns. I can say it was Bible stories, my mother would say, my Children give your lives to Jesus but I would answer her, mum, your dress is very big when Jesus comes I will hide inside and go with you. My mother answered, Betty, I love you and I love all my children, but in heaven I will go alone. My mother would take time to teach us and to explain the word of God to us but still I did not believe in God. My heart was just hard, oh my mother! But I had my reasons why I couldn't believe. In my heart I said to her, how can you love God and God loves you but you suffer too much like this! Because I had watched my mother being beaten by my father, making her to sleep in the bush like an animal. It was hard to believe that God love her. My question was, if Jesus is there why can't He help you! I believe my mother's teaching at that time was going out side my ears but entering my heart. As I was growing that seed was there, within me I had that witness in my heart that Jesus really loved me. Back in Uganda I had given my life to Jesus but later dropped out, after coming to UK. In as much I was hearing God, I could still hear my mother's voice but she had died a long time! My mother's favourite lessons and messages in the Bible were how God saved a prophet named Jonah from the belly of a fish, Jonah 1: 1 to end. How God saved Daniel from the lion's den, Daniel 6: 10-23. The three Hebrews, Daniel's friends Shadrach, Meshach and Abed-nego whom king Nebuchadnezzar threw in the fiery furnace (fire) because they had refused to worship his a golden image and how God delivered them, Daniel 3: 1-18. My mother knew how to do that, I thank God who had blessed me with God fearing mother. I said that I will also do the same to my son but inseated my son has taken my mother's (his grandmother) character, it's so amazing I, can call it blood transfusion! Everything that was in my late mother, the worship, hunger for the souls and to preach the Gospel. Sometime I look and wonder how my son runs after souls, then I know my mother really left a seed behind. When I sat in the room those days in 2011, I could hear my mother's messages playing in my head, no matter how I tried to run I couldn't escape Jesus' love, no matter how I couldn't get away. His love was rather chasing after me! It's like a magnet you can't escape. Inside my heart I knew I had tasted Jesus' love but out of stupidity because of what I faced in UK, I shifted my love from Him but at the end it was salt in the wound. I can't believe that it's now 2020 and I decided to type my message and writing I started eight years ago! I kept in the big note book! When I got this inspiration to write I went and bought that big note book. I knew I heard a message, English was my problem but I started any way. With my pen I wrote and wrote, then I reached half way I kept. OK one pastor (lady) who knew that I was writing asked me in 2018 if I had finished and published this book because I used to ask her for help if I got word or a dream and lacked interpretation or meaning. Twice I took my big note book to her house so she could correct me. She willingly corrected some of my English mistakes with more encouragements. I openly told her that I did not have education but I had a message. But almost half way through it, her family relocated to East London. I kept on writing I did not stop then in a few months one lady joined the church where I worshipped after I had learned that she was a lawyer, I got close to her and asked if she was able to help me! She corrected a few mistakes, then I decided to stop writing. I was very annoyed I wanted to throw the book away because it was too messy but inseated I dumped somewhere. During lock down period (COVID-19) as my son and I, were at home I decided to resume, I started from where I had stopped eight years ego. I don't know what happened but the message went to a different direction which I did not plan. I think I started all over again, I could have kept two per cent of what I started with eight years ago. I can tell that my English is not as it was in 2012, I have gained more understanding I'm even correcting myself! Even though I had dumped that big not book somewhere, I had never stopped writing it in my head. I remember the dream I dreamt in that season when God visited me in the night and told me, I have given you the gift of writing! Another voice came and told me, I, give you the hand writing of the holy sprit! To me I think things of God are actually out sense in some ways! I had never dreamt that one day I would author a book, I never thought that one day I would be able to write a book! Yes, when I was a child my first and foremost dream was to be a secretary (typist!) Where I had to be in the office just writing because I loved writing. But then my dream was terminated due to lack of education. I kept on meditating on the word, *hand writing of the holy sprit! What does it mean? Then one day my elven years old son told me, mum, do you know that God actually supports your hands!* Any way I decided to write, practice makes perfect. To make the knife sharp you have to sharpen it all time otherwise it will grow blunt. This is was my first book but I had put it a side. I have been meditating on in it, every thing I was doing. I was writing it and editing it in my head. When this pastor asked me if I had done something with it, I, answered, no! But somehow she woke me. "She told me, you have kept that message sister Betty! She asked, Do you know why God decided to give that message to you? That question bothered me! I wrote a book out of confusion, so how can it be that it was God who inspired me! I did not want to ask her this question. But this God looked for un educated woman to give her the message! I thought I was writing through my experiences? So what happened to me, was an intention? When my child was a baby, early years children centre was offering some short courses, Mathematics and English. I did English and writing, five weeks short course for those who did not know English but I failed to get my certificate. I can say that I was looking to make it perfect but how can you perfect what you are not practicing! In some way, I'm calling this book, ***lock down book, the power of lock down, I locked myself in and finally wrote this book that had been dumped somewhere for eight years!*** Those days when I used to clean the building where we had a church at that time, while I was cleaning I heard this song rating through my head: "*Oh sweet Jesus, oh sweet Jesus, beautiful love sweet caring darling Jesus, I worship you!* **Beautiful love,** to beautiful love, Beautiful God,

1John 4: 8, he who does not love does not know God for God is love. So if God is love do we understand what we say when we say, I love you! Or there is another type of love? I leave it for Pastors to explain! But then I jumped into conclusion and said, may be there is earthly love which has become a type of greeting, I'm just imagining! I did not say, it is! God cares, may be that is why I was getting that song. *sweet caring darling Jesus!* When you sing out of a broken heart! Ehe.. I received that song titled Rose of Sharoni I looked for meaning, what I got was, Rose of Sharon is a beautiful flower, it does not fade:

You are the beautiful flowers that never fades,
Rose of Sharon I worship you! I worship you
I worship you, I bow down for you, I worship you.
You the Master planner that never fails.
Rose of Sharon, I worship you. I worship you,
I worship you, I bow down for you, I worship you.

You are the beautiful creator that Best artists,
Rose of Sharon, I worship you. I worship you,
I worship you, I bow down for you, I worship you.

This song was conceived when homelessness caused me to wander around. As I was wandering, going where I did not know, I was worshipping at the same time. Then I saw a very beautiful flower, still singing and admiring that beautiful flower a song came to my mouth and it was worth it. Jesus' love never changes and never fades. My God-Jesus, you are so beautiful and you will never change, you are the only living God, so why can't I praise you, why cant I worship you just for your love?

Beautiful God I worship you,
Beautiful God I worship you,
I honour you and adore you.
For you are holy, you are holy Jesus.

I can call this this book read as you praise, read as you sing. Appreciating God's love towards me has also made me to write. When I couldn't understand and I had to sing my questions to Him! I started by saying, who am I?

Who am I, Jesus, who am I, who am I,
who am I, Jesus, that you love me like this?
Your love for me, Jesus, I cannot understand it!
And I don't know what I did, that you love like this!

This song is titled, our God is so good:

Our God is so good, our God is so good,
Our God is so good, He has done us great things,
Our God is so good,
Come, let us praise Him, come, let us praise Him, come let us praise Him,
Our God is so good
Come let us thank Him, come let us thank Him, come let thank Him,
Our God is good.
Talk abut His goodness, talk about His love, talk about His saving hand,
Our God is so good.

Talk about His sweetness, sweeter, sweeter than honey,
sweeter, sweeter than sugar, Our God is good.

Will you sing with me this song?

Will you sing with me this song? Will you sing with me this song?
Will you sing with me this song?
I love, I love the Lord,
I love, I love the Lord,
I love, I love the Lord.
He paid the price I could not pay! He paid the price I could not pay!
He paid all debts I could not pay!
I love, I love the Lord,
I love, I love the Lord,
I love, I love the Lord.
He is a God that cannot fail, He is a God that cannot fail,
He is a God that cannot fail.
I love, I love the Lord,
I love, I love the Lord,
I love, I love the Lord.
He hates sin, He loves sinners, He loves sinners,
He hates sin, but He loves sinners.
I love, I love the Lord,
I love, I love the Lord,
I love, I love the Lord.
He is the way the truth and life, He is the way the truth and life,
He is the way the truth and life.
I love, I love the Lord,
I love, I love the Lord,
I love, I love the Lord.
Will you sing with me this song, I love, I love the Lord.

Devine mercy

It's been eight years when I wrote this testimony I can still remember I was in that small my room where my son and I lived. I still remember how our lives were, I started by saying: " I want to give thank Jesus who washed my sins away, because it's not easy living without Jesus. Living a life without Jesus is like spending the rest of your life carrying a heavy stone on your head! Just imagine a heavy stone on your head every day. That is how I was but came to a point where I got tired. Then I said, enough is enough I can't continue like this, I knew that Jesus loves me, I knew that the blood that Jesus shed has power to wash my sins and take those regrets away from my heart. At some point it did not make sense to me, I had gone through many challenges but I was still standing. For sure it was not me who kept my life going but it was God who kept me, it was love, God Himself is love,

I had created anger for myself out of disappointments and it became my worst enemy, I had searched for love in wrong places. I was running from the rain and eventually I hide myself under a tree and that tree where I went to hide had no leaves! I was desperately looking to get happiness from a wrong corner, the story changed when God decided to visit me. It was 4/2/ 2011, I went to sleep as I about waking up in the morning, in my dream I saw someone coming towards me He was dressed in white, He touched me and said," divine mercy, I did not doubt I knew it was Jesus. The reason I was in a shared accommodation is because I had just been disappointed and became a single mother! That very weekend, Sunday we went to church then a pastor preached as if he knew what I was going through! Quietly I started asked myself, can I go home like this again? As I was still talking to myself pastor asked, he made an altar call. I put up my hand and walked to the front and he prayed for me. At that time I felt so light, for I had been very heavy. From that time I started reading my Bible more and more for myself and for my son. Before that, things were horrible. I introduced my three years old son to worship, I started exposing him to great worshippers since we had a You tube channel. My baby started talking about God, before he went to bed in night he would say sleep with me Jesus, in the morning he would say good morning Jesus. I was hurting myself trying to catch what had already fallen. Sorry you can't catch that bird that flies in air unless you have wings to. I knew that in Him and in His name I could find strength. I was in bondage, like a woman at the well I was seeking for......! But Jesus said, *Philippians 5:7, cast all your care upon me for I care about you.*

Psalm 55:22, cast your cares upon the Lord and He will sustain you. So all I, needed was to call on Jesus. Saviour of the world. Happiness is not purchased with any money. Jesus has power to save those in bondage and to strengthen those who are weak. The thirsty will drink from the river of life.

Revelation 21:6, and He said to me, it is done! I am Alpha and Omega, the beginning and the End. I will give of the fountain o f the water of life freely to him who thirsts,

(NKJV.

(NIV, He said to me, it is done! I am the Alpha and Omega, the Beginning and the End. To the thirsty I will give water without cost from the spring of the water of Life.

Matthew 5:6, Blessed are those who hunger and thirst for righteousness for they shall be filled.

There is a song I love, I'm sure the author will not mind that I borrowed it after all we are making Jesus contagious. We have to spread Him across. let your living water flow over my soul:

Let your living water flow over my soul.
Let your Holy spirit come and take control.
Of every situation that has troubled my mind.
All my cares and burdens onto you, I roll.

Jesus, Jesus, Jesus. (chorus)
Father, Father, Father.
Spirit, Spirit, Spirit.
Come now Holy Spirit and take control.
Keep me in your loving arms and make me whole.
Wipe away all doubts and fear and take my pride.

Draw me to your love and keep me by your side.
Chorus)
Give your life to Jesus,
Let Him fill your soul.
Let Him take you in His loving arms and make you whole.
As you give your life to Him, He will set you free.
You will live and reign with Him eternally.
Chorus)

My mother loved this hymn:

Shall we gather at the river
Where bright Angele feet have trod,
With its crystal tide forever
Flowing by the throne of God?

Yes, we will gather at the river,
The beautiful, the beautiful river
Gather with the saints at the river
Flowing by the throne of God.

On the margin of the river,
Washing up its silver spray,
We will talk and worship ever,
All the happy golden day.

(Chorus) Yes, we will gather at the river,
The beautiful, the beautiful river,
Gather with saints at the river
Flowing by the throne of God.
Ere, we reach the shining river,
We lay every burden down,
Grace our spirits will deliver
And provide a robe and crown
(Chorus)

At the shining of the river
Mirror of the Saviours face
Saints whom death will never sever
Lift their song of saving grace.
(Chorus)
Soon we will reach the silver river
Soon our pilgrimage will cease
Soon our hearts will quiver
With the melody of peace.
(Chorus)

One woman met with Jesus face to face and He told her the same word, she was thirsty and searching, but she got more than what she wanted! River of the living *water.*

John 7:37, on the last day of the great feast, Jesus stood and cried out saying, if anyone is thirsty let him come and drink.

There is this thirsty that we create for ourselves! We tend to thirsty for these things that add no value, as if one wants to carry the whole world! But then I thought that there is this type, when you can't live Jesus alone. One is thirsty for nothing, another is thirsty for Jesus, *Matthew 6:33, He said: seek first the Kingdom of God and His righteousness and all these things shall be added to you.*

Lord I thirsty for you, I want to be in your presence.
My soul will wait on you.
Father draw near to the beauty of your holiness.
And I will wait on you and I will worship you.
In the beauty of your holiness.

My understanding, to be thirsty for Jesus, is when I, want to be in His presence all the time, worshipping Him, reading the Bible. You can be in in His presence whenever and wherever. *Psalm 16-11, You show me the path of life, in your presence is fullness of joy, at your right hand are pleasures for* ***evermore****.*

Psalms 91:1, He who dwells in the secret place of the Most High, shall abide under the shadow of the Almighty.

I personal don't love cold water (fridge water) no matter how thirsty I am! If I'm too thirsty and I make a mistake of drinking water from the fridge, my thirsty will not be quenched. If I go to buy a drink in the corner shop I always ask, can I, please have a warm one! I mean, the one out of the fridge! But hen I would not want anything to quench my thirst for Jesus, after I have received Him. I want Him more and more, that is when I can have fridge water because I don't want to be quenched at all. I want to be like a deer, I want to Pant after God, to Pant after that living water.

Psalms 42:1-2, As deer Pants for the water Brooks, pants my soul pants for you, O God. My soul thirsts for God, for the living God.

Those who hasn't received Jesus as their Lord and saviour come and drink, from the well that never runs dry. Jesus is the living well. One might ask, how can I, drink Jesus? Do I use a cup to draw Him? Where I come from, (village) we often fetch water from the well. If someone needs water has to go out and fetch from the well. Because it's not as same as living in cities where we have water in the houses. In my village, your water will run out then someone will have to go back to the well, again and again! Now this is Jesus, the living water, if you have him you know that you have more than a drink. Who wants to run round with a bucket when you can have the river in your own compound? If you have Jesus, you can never carry your bucket around looking for water again. Because we often we run, here and there seeking for what we want and after we have found just what we had been searching for, we don't seen to be satisfied. It's seems as if there is a hole within us craving for more.

Now when we read the Gospel of John we will understand because there also was a Samaritan woman who was always thirsty, she was never satisfied. She was searching everywhere.

John 4:6, now Jacob's well was there, Jesus therefore being wearied from His journey sat thus by the well, it was about the six hours.

-V7, a woman of Samaria came to draw water, Jesus said to her, give me a drink!

-Van 9, the woman answered, and said to Him (Jesus) how is it that you being a Jew ask a drink from me, a Samaritan woman?" For Jews have no dealing with Samarians?

She did not know that she finally found a saviour, she refused to give Jesus a drink. That is why she held tight to her bucket. She had no idea that the Man she was speaking with happened to be *Jesus!* Though her eye were about to be opened, Jesus said to her,

-V10, Jesus answered, (her) and said, "if you knew the gift of God and He who it is who say to you, "Give me a drink, 'you would have asked Him and He would have given you living water.

I'm sure she looked at Jesus and said, man, you don't even have the bucket! How dare you say can give me living water, and what is living water anyway?

-V11, the woman said to Him, "Sir,you have nothing to draw with and the well is deep. Where then do you get that living water?

But this woman was determined to argue this case with a Man whom she did not know!

Would you believe that this woman asked Jesus if He was greater than her ancestor? She was descendant of Jacob.

In John 4:12, she continued, are you greater than our father Jacob, who gave us this well and drink from it himself, as well as his sons his Livestock?

Jesus looked kindly at her!

-V13-14, Jesus answered (her) and said to her whoever drinks of this water will thirsty again. but whoever drinks of the water that I shall give him will never thirsty, but the water that I, give him will become in him a fountain of water springing up into everlasting life.

The woman thought living water was the best idea and said,

-V15, the woman to Him (Jesus) Sir give me this water that I may not thirsty again, nor come here to draw."

-V16, Jesus, said to her, "go, call your husband and come here.

My friends, tell me was this woman in UK or in Samaria? I bet she did not use these men one by one to get a UK Visa (red passport) women remember when you insulted me that the reason I did not have a UK visa was because I did not have wisdom to use a men so I could get a visa and money from them? You told me that a *wise* woman is that woman who uses a man to get money, to get visa then as soon you get what you want you live him! Remember when you said, *no wonder you have no wisdom*! I admit that the love I had for my son's father was real, and not after Visa or money and for sure I got my confession! Be careful how you say things! I can still hear them say, you better look for a man who will give you a visa! My answer, was, I not run after a man because of his money or because he has a UK visa, but whom my heart loves! A woman asked me, what can this poor man from Ghana give you? He came to England to work just like you! I answered, that woman, for your information, this man is not poor and I, told these advisers to leave me alone! After there were all wrong a hundred times! A wise woman is not that one who uses men. In fact there were using evil mind to push me into the pit but they met with me!

John 4:17, the woman answered, and said, I have no husband, "Jesus said to her, you have well said, I, have no husband.

V18, Jesus, said to her, you have had five husbands and the one whom you now have is not your husband, in that you have spoken well.

V19-20, the woman said to Jesus, Sir, I perceive you are a prophet, our fathers worshipped on this mountain but you Jews you say that in Jerusalem is the place one ought to worship."

V21, Jesus said to her," Woman, believe me the hour is coming when you will neither on this mountain or in Jerusalem worship the Father.

V23, Jesus said to her, the hour is coming and now is when the true worshippers will worship the Father in spirit and in truth, for the Father is seeking such to worship Him.

V24, God is a spirit and those who worship Him must worship in spirit and in truth.

V25, the woman said to Jesus, I know that Messiah is coming, who is called Christ, when He comes He will tell us all things.

V26, Jesus said to her, I, who speaks to you, I am He.

I'm imagining, at this moment Jesus looking at this woman with love while saying to her, daughter, I am not who you think Iam! I AM the living water. If you lift your pot I will fill it, drink from me and quench your thirsty. I should think that her plan was, " I kick out the one I have, and this one will come in! Jesus knew how she previously had five husbands or should I should I say **used** five husbands to satisfy her needs. Use this man, if it the case, *who* told you that men are not experts in using women to get UK visa! This language does sound **ugly** you know! But she was still searching, Jesus knew what her next plan was. Because Jesus knew the time she came to fetch water, He came and waited for her! And when she came looking for man number seven she found A MAN Jesus sitting by the well, He said to her, it's time to rest my daughter. You have had enough I know! You are the reason I came, we need to talk.

Matthew 11:28, come to me all you who labour and heavy laden and I, will give you rest.

The woman got more than what she was looking for, I can Imagine, if she was cooking and had left a pot on fire the time she spent chatting with Jesus (Man) was too long! I guess that food got burnt! But never mind! She did not go home straight, because she left her water pot and went to evangelise. God is ready to use any one, from being a husband snatcher or men user to becoming an evangelist!

-V28-29, the woman left her water pot, went her into the city and said to the men,

"come and see a Man who told me all things that I ever did. Could this be the Christ?"

Because she had already asked Jesus a question, same chapter- V 19, Sir I perceive you are a prophet!

I wonder what came to her mind at that moment when Jesus told her, I am Christ whom you have been waiting for! She couldn't keep it to herself. She must share Jesus with others! She went to evangelise, she went proclaim Jesus to others.

-V30, then they went out to of the city and came to Him.

I can't imagine, what came to that woman's mind when she first set her eyes on Jesus! From the beginning she saw a man, but Jesus turned out to be different from six men. Could it be that it was the same place where Jesus was. But this time no man came! Only JESUS! I guess women from that town were tired of her. *Do you think the men she snatched were single men or they had families?* A MAN Jesus changed her life for good. At last she found rest in Him. The woman came to draw and found Jesus the living well.

Her testimony brought others to Jesus, who could have testified to the whole town? Because of her many Samaritans believed in Jesus.

Saviour of the world.

John 4:39, and many Samaritans of that city believed in Him because of the word of the woman who testified, "He told me all that ever did.

-V4o, So when the Samaritans had come to Him, they urged Him to stay to stay there two days.

-V41, And many more believed because of His own word.

V42, they said to the woman, "Now, we believe not because of what you said, for we have heard for our selves and know that this indeed is Christ, the Saviour of the world.

Jesus, the water of life.

There is an invitation to abundant life in *Isaiah 55 : 1-3, it says, ho! Everyone who is thirsty, come to the waters; and you who has no money, come, buy and eat. Yes come buy wine and milk without money and without price.*

2, why do you spend money for what is not bread and your wages for what does not satisfy? Listen diligently to me and eat what is good and let your soul delight itself in abundance.

3, Listen carefully to me, and eat what is good, and your soul delight itself in abundance.

Writing songs one day, I received this song:

We have come to the river of abundance.
We have come to the river of abundance.
There is healing, there is healing, in the river of abundance.
There is deliverance, there is deliverance, in the river of abundance.
There is salvation, there salvation, in the river of abundance.
There is breakthrough, there is breakthrough, in the river of abundance.
There is rest, there is rest, in the river of abundance.
There is peace, there is peace, in the river of abundance.
We have to the river of abundance.
End.

Jesus, I love your love in a such way that I cannot even explain, this brings me to the next song:

"Oh Jesus, you love me, I know, I know you love Daddy,
Oh Jesus you love me, I know, I know, you care about me.
Oh Jesus, I will praise you,
Oh Jesus, I will honour you Father,
Oh Jesus, I adore you, because I know you care about me.
So let me dance for you, so let me dance for you,
So let me dance you, I know, I know you care about me.

Jesus' love is so amazing, Jesus demonstrated His love to us by dying on the cross,

Acts 17:3, explaining and demonstrating that the Christ had to suffer and rise again from the dead saying, "This Jesus who I preach to you is the Christ.

Matthew 27:50, when Jesus, had cried out again with a loud voice, yielded up His spirit.

Who can die for a friend? But Jesus did, a friend of sinners is Jesus, He was crucified with two robbers.

Mark 15:27, Along with Jesus, they crucified two robbers, one on His right hand and one His left.

Mark 15:28, And the scripture was fulfilled, which says, and He was numbered with transgressors.

Luke 22:37, Jesus said, for I say to you that this which is written must be accomplished in me: and He was number with transgressors, for the things concerning me have an end.

Isaiah 53:12 b, Because He poured out his soul into death, and He was numbered with transgressors.

I enjoy writing songs about Jesus, I enjoy talking about Jesus' love to us. Jesus a friend of sinners, a hater of sin:

"Jesus a friend of sinners, He was nailed on the cross,
Jesus our Saviour, Jesus our Saviour, He was nailed on the cross,
Jesus a friend of sinners.
Because of His love He died to save us, He died to save us,
Jesus a friend of sinners,
See how He was beaten, the Crown of thorns on His head, He was crucified with robbers,
Jesus a friend of sinners,
See how He is calling, come to me you sinners, come to me I love you,
Jesus a friend of sinners.
Say no to satan receive the love of Jesus, receive the love of Jesus,
Jesus a friend of sinners.
Nothing can wash our sins except the blood of Jesus, which He shed at Calvary,
Jesus a friend of sinners.
Dip yourself in His blood, dip yourself in His blood
Jesus a friend of sinners.
End.

The blood of Jesus has power to wash our sins, to cleanse us and set captive free. As the song says, indeed, nothing can wash our sins except the blood of Jesus, which He shed at Calvary.

1 Peter 1:19, But with the precious blood of Christ as of a Lamb without blemish and without spot.

1John 1:7, but if we walk in light as He is in the light, we have fellowship with one another and the blood of Jesus Christ His Son cleanses us from all sins.

Hebrews 9:22, and according to the law, almost all things are purged with blood and within shedding of blood there is no remission.

Hebrews 9:12, not with the blood of goat and calves but with His own blood Jesus entered the most Holy place once and for all, having obtained eternal redemption.

Matthew 26:28, for this is my blood of the new testament, which is shed for many for the remission of sins.

Isaiah 1:18, Come now let us reason together," says the Lord, "Though your sins are scarlet, they shall be as whiter as snow, though they are red like crimson, they shall be as wool.

Jesus died for me:

Jesus died for me, Jesus died for me,
Jesus died for me, He died to set me free.
Hallelujah, my saviour died for me,
My saviour died for me, my saviour died for me
He died, to wash my sins away,
He died, to wash my sins away.
End.

Another song:

see the King of glory who once was dead, He's alive forever more,
see the King of glory who once was dead, He's alive forever more.
He defeated satan, He defeated satan, He defeated satan,
He's alive forever more.
The crown of thorns turned out to be the crown of glory,
He's is alive forever more.
End.

I was receiving such songs, I wrote the Tomb is empty:

Hallelujah, Hallelujah, Hallelujah Amen,
The stone had been rolled away,
the stone had been rolled away.
He's alive, He's alive, Jesus is risen,
He's alive He's alive, Jesus is risen.
The Tomb is empty, Jesus is risen,
The tomb is empty, Jesus is risen.
Bow on your knees and worship Him.
Bow on your knees and worship Him,
He's alive, He's alive, Jesus is risen.
End.

Look up

It is a beautiful to hear God's voice, it is so amazing and His voice is so sweet, I can say again that I have been blessed to hear God's voice. He comes in my dreams to teach me. I could be sleeping and all of a sudden I hear my sprit singing a new song. One Sunday morning I woke up with these words in my mouth,

The power of God is so might, the power of God is so mighty!

In the same dream, I was singing a song about a man in the Bible who was paralysed for thirty eight years. The one who was sitting by the pool. John 5:1-14, in my dream it's like I could see angles coming to star water, others would quickly jump in. It was like seeing movie. In that dream I wrote song:

Do you want to be healed? Jesus is asking,
Jesus is asking, Jesus is waiting, come to Jesus.

When I woke up, I wrote the dream down. Still in 2012, my baby and I went out to the park, as we were there I received a song but this song came as an assurance, it was a word from God:

Jesus, Jesus strong solid Rock,
Even though I stumble I will get up again.

One night I received a phone call of eviction, My baby was sleeping at that time I looked at him and in my heart I said, where will I put you? I became very troubled I wanted to say something but inseated I cried and went to sleep, but I was sleeping that night I heard a voice saying clearly saying, "***look up, don't let you heart be troubled, John 14 : 1,*** waking up from sleep, I said thank you Lord and forgive me not trusting you. For sure that eviction plan was cancelled at that time because God intervened. See, I did not say anything with my mouth but God perceived my thoughts and came through four us. We can't hide anything from God. He knows our hearts and He knows what we need, if we ask Him and trust

Him, He will give us our heart's desire. God is our Father He did not create us to suffer. He is Kind to His children, we know how we approach our earthly father, when you need some things. I can't say that God, our heavenly Father is on the same level with our earthly fathers, He is higher than the highest, but to make the point clear we shouldn't just come to God and all we say is give me, give me! What about if we give God what He can't give to Himself, just adore Him. I can say just give Him that adoration because you love Him. May be the reason I'm saying it because it has worked for me. Praise Him, sing out your love to Him, give thanks to Him and worship Him for who He is, not for what you want from Him. Those days that I called ugly days, in that mad shared accommodation I was writing songs like a crazy woman. When I hated my situation but I loved the fact that I was breathing, I remember receiving a song in my sprit:

Every day of my life, everyday of my life, (chorus)
I will say thank you Jesus.
When I look around me,
I see the reason to be so-so, grateful.
Jesus, are so- good to me,
You have been so-so good to me.

Chorus) Every day of my life, every day of my life.
I will say thank you Jesus.

I have many, many reasons to be so-so grateful.
Jesus, I cannot count all my blessings.
There are too much for me to talk about,
Jesus, what shall I ever give you? Only to worship you,
Everyday of my life, I will say thank you Jesus.

Chorus) Every day of my life, every day of my life.
I will say thank you Jesus.
End.

Betty Amiina

I received a song like this, in the days I called dark ugly days! Some songs are prophetic, if a song comes to you, just received it the way it is because it can be a word of for you. I try not change anything in case I tamper with it or dilute it. In my corner when my father was very sick back in Uganda, I worshipped God for who He is. I was thanking God instead of asking. My visa had a restriction on at that time but I was not restricted to sing praises to God! In fact having no visa on the other hand gave me more time to worship. I was not running around to look for Jobs, or waking up early to go to work. I used that time to worship God then in the fullness of time my visa showed up. In 2017 December my son and I were able to travel to Uganda and see my father. OK, he later passed away in October 2018 but I was so grateful to God in a way that my son had a chance to see his grandfather. Grateful to see that at the time my father died I already had my visa otherwise I couldn't have attended his funeral. From 2010, when my father became sick God was working, but I think I wanted microwave style! I would look at my son and talking to myself I would then say, don't worry Isaiah, God will surely do it, you will see your grandfather! Even my father refused to give me a break, whenever called to greet him he would ask me, Betty, when are you intending to bring my grand son? My father would add, I'm waiting for my grand son to bless him before I die! My father's question and statements bothered my heart so I refused to give God rest! I had longed to see my father! If I had prayed, I decided to switch to worship, from the time I put my mind to worship God, I began to hear Him audibly and I'm not even a prophet! And so what I saw in my dream concerning my father came to pass. God even me showed the type clothes my father would be wearing! I a dream I saw my father in a blue pyjamas and he was walking with a stick. God! My father was wearing a striped pyjamas, blue, white and green colours! With my two eyes, I saw my father wearing those pyjamas colours and he was walking in the compound with a stick! It was too much for me. At that time I was standing in my stepmother's compound, as my walked towards me I was so happy, it was amazing, I wanted to scream but! It was exactly how I saw my father in the dream back in 2011. I think God said, Betty, let me show you what I had showed you. This God works with His timetable but I was pushing. My son and I, made it to the glory of God, my son's mission was to win his grandfather for Jesus, as soon we finished greeting my father my son looked at him and asked, granddad, have you ever received Jesus in Your heart? My son said, granddad, I want to pray for you to receive Jesus. Then my father said, pray for me my child, then my son laid his hand on him and prayed a prayer of salvation, thus my son won his grandfather for Jesus. Then my son asked, granddad, how old are you? At a time my father was eighty six. And my son was eight years old. Sometimes all we have to do is, to leave God do His work because He knows how put things in order for us. Never a late God, always on time. But I call Him late God on purpose, intentionally. I came to a conclusion that every thing I wanted Him to do for my father and to do for me during my father's sickness is because He is God and He is able. God loves our worship, He is refreshed when He hears worship. **I *wrote this song.***

Jesus sweet God, Jesus sweet God.
Delicious Jesus, I really love you.
Delicious Jesus, I really love you.
I have come to worship you Jesus.
To fall down at your feet.
To tell how beautiful you are,
Sweet Jesus, you are so wonderful
Sweet Jesus, you are so wonderful.

I will bow and worship you Jesus.
At your feet I will humble crawl.
I will break my alabaster for you.
Oh Jesus, this is how much I love you.
Oh Jesus, this is how much I love you.

I will praise and worship you.
I will give honour Lord.
I will break my alabaster for you.
Oh Jesus, this is how much I love you.
Oh Jesus, this is how much I love you.
End.

Love came from glory

God's favourite! God loves us, God loves each and every one, Jesus a friend of sinners. His love to humanity nailed Him to the cross, coming all the way from heaven He was looking for you and me. My son always tells me, Mum, in the whole school my favourite teacher is this! Mum of all my of all my uncles, uncle so- is one of my favourite, then he goes on to say but mum I love them all very much! So if you love them all, why uncle that particular uncle is the favourite one? Because he carried me on his shoulder! He asked, mum do you remember when we were going to greet his friends and he carried me, he put on his shoulder to cross the bridge? My son's uncle earned he favouritism because of one thing, he carried me! Can I say that God has favourites? In as much as I know that there is no favouritism with God, Romans 2:11, *for God shows no favouritism, NIV). For there is no partiality with God, (NKJV.* In this I can say that God has favourites. Can God treat us the same, though He love us all? When you become born again, do you become a child of God and also His favourite? That is what I thought. When I was planning to write this book I was obsessed with it, I wanted to know, who are God's favourites? I know God loves us all but does He have His favourites! Who are God's favourite children! Then I said, I'm sure God has His favourite! in blacket, I said, those who are close to Him. That child that is close to Him, that child who loves to be in His father's presence, always worshipping Him. That child who love to please Him, reading and studying His word! *Children of God, who are they?* Those who choose to follow Jesus as their Lord and personal saviour, those who say, I divorce you satan, you devil, from today I turn away from your ways I want follow Jesus alone. Those who say, satan, I no longer walk with you, Jesus is the only Master over my life. Say to that devil, I, no longer serve you, I want to become a child of God. because when you surrender your live to Jesus you, automatically become a child of God. Something tell me that we are all God's creation but we are not all God's children. **But** I want to be called a child of God, then surrender your life you Jesus! *Children of God will you shout Hallelujah?* **Wether God has favourites remains a question to me. Bible scholars will help me to know if God has favourite children but in my opinion I said, I, think I can go**

an extra length to earn that from God! My elven years old son told me that **God can't have favourites because God loves all His children equally. He added, God can't exalt one child above the other! I, asked him again, so why does Bible say that Abraham was a friend of God?** *James 2 :23, and the scripture was fulfilled which says, " Abraham believed God and it was accounted to him for righteousness and was called* a *friend* of God! **The my son answered, a friend is not a favourite. God does hate sin but He loves sinners, He loves His people! He almost confused me, when he talked about people of God and children of God!** So I remembered a verse, *2 chronicles 7:14, if my people who are called by my name will humble themselves and pray and seek my face and turn from their wicked way ways then I will hear from heaven, and I will forgive their sins and heal their land!* I pondered on this verse but **my son ask me?** *Do you know what it means to be a child of God?* Imagine you being a child of the Most High God! **Then I said,** I'm sure very one would love to be called a child of God! A singer sang this song:

I'm no longer a slave to fear, I'm a child of God!

So that means that we are slaves before children of God! Which means if you don't receive Jesus in your heart you remain a slave? A slave for the rest of your life! A slave to satan, but you don't need to remain in slavery because **Love** paid it all, He paid a full price with His blood to free you and me from slavery and to redeem us back to Good. *Revelation 5:9, you are worthy to take the scroll and open its seals, for you were slain and redeemed back to God by your blood.*

Colossians 1:14, In whom we have redemption through His blood, even the forgiveness of sins.

Ephesians 1:7, In Him we have redemption through His blood, the forgiveness of our trespasses, according to His riches of His grace.

Titus 2:14, Who gave Himself for us that He might redeemer us from every lawless deed and purify for Himself His own special people zealous for good works.

There is nothing more expensive than the blood of Jesus, nothing so precious than the blood of Jesus! Jesus put everything upon His shoulders because of love, I have a song:

I have a Father His name is Jesus.
Mighty in battle, Jehovah Nissi.
In times of trouble, He is my defender.
He will never, never leave me.
He will never forsake me.
Ever present God, always with me,
How can not love you Jesus?
how can I not love you?
How can I not love you?
How can I not love you?
Your love for me took you to Calvary
To die for me, to die for me.
Where can I go, from your presence?
I have no other God.
Who is like you, ready to catch me,
In case I fall down

Oh sweet, sweet Jesus.
How can I ever forget,
how you suffered for me on the hill Calvary!

My Redeemer Jesus, you died to set me free,
How can ever forget!
How you suffered for me, on the hill Calvary!.
A friend of sinners, you are full of love.
how can I ever forget,
how you suffered for me, on the hill Calvary!
End.

We need to show our gratitude to our Lord Jesus because of what He went through for us, He suffered, *Hebrews 13:12, and Jesus also suffered outside the city gate to make the people holy through His blood.*

All the beating, that big cross which He carried, they spat on His face, *Matthew 27:30, When they had spat on Him, and took the reed and struck Him on the head.*

They stripped off His clothes, *Matthew 27:28, and they stripped Him and put a Scarlet rob on Him.*

They put a crown of thorn on Him, *Matthew 27:29, when they had twisted a crown of thorns they put it on His head and Reed in His right hand and bowed their knees before Him and mocked Him saying, hail King of Jews.*

They later hanged Him on a tree, *Matthew 27:35, and when they crucified Him, they divided His clothes by casting lots.*

They left Him there to die, *Matthew 27:50, When Jesus had cried out again with a loud voice, He yielded up His spirit.*

John 19:30, so when Jesus had received a sour wine He said, it is finished!" And bowed His head, He gave up His spirit.

Still on a tree they pieced His body, *John 19:34, but one of the soldiers pierced His side with a spear and immediately blood and water came out.*

Jesus went through a lot for us, what a saviour! He died an ugly shameful death! what manner of love? All the way from glory just to die like! His mission was accomplished,

John 19:28, after this Jesus knowing that all things were accomplished, that the scriptures that might be fulfilled, said, I thirsty.

His last words were," *It's finished, John 19:30.*

When Jesus had lived on earth for thirty three years He finished all that the came to do. Out of love God sent Jesus His only beloved son into the world to die just for us!

John 3:16, for God so loved the world that He sent His only begotten son that whoever believes in Him should not perish but have eternal life.

17th *verse, God did not send His son into the world to condemn the world but that through Him the world might be saved.*

Writing songs I, wrote this short song: *Light of the world shine before me, I want to see my way Jesus, take me to gates of heaven.*

Jesus came into this world to show us the way to heaven, He came to show us the way to the father. His death brought reconciliation.

2 Corinthians 5 v18, and now all things are of God, who has reconciled us to Himself through Jesus Christ.

Before Jesus, there was no way for us to heaven, we had no access to God, there was a big wall between us and God. Adam's sin had brought separation but through Jesus we were reunited, Hallelujah! My elven years old son puts it this way, ***Jesus opened the gate for us to go to heaven. He made way for us to enter.*** Jesus is a path way.

John 14:6, I'm the ***way*** *the truth and life,* ***no one comes to the father except through me****.* Again Jesus said, I am the door, *John* 10:9, *I am the door if anyone enters by me, he will be saved.*

Those hours that Jesus was on the cross darkness filled the land, but why did it happen?

Matthew 27 v45, from noon until three in the afternoon dark came over all the land.

Matthew 27 v51, at that moment the curtain of the temple was torn in two from top to bottom. The earth shook, the rocks sprit,

v52 and the tombs broke open. The bodies of many holy people who died were raised to life.

I remember when Jesus told Martha in *John 11 v25, Jesus said to her, "I'm the resurrection and life.*

Back to Matthew *27 v53, and coming out of the grave after Jesus' resurrection they went into the holy city and appeared to many*

I just realised that Jesus was on the cross three hours and He also was in the tomb three days, but what was he really doing there?

Matthew 27 very 59, and Joseph had taken the body he wrapped it in a clean linen cloth.

Matthew 27 v63-66, Sir we remember will he was still alive this deceiver said, after three days I will rise again,

64, therefore command that that the tomb be made secure lest His disciples should come at night and still Him away and say to the people, He is risen from the dead. So the last deception will be worse than the first. Palate said to the me, you have a guard, go you way, make it as secure as you know how to. They went and made the tomb secure, sealing the stone and setting the guard.

But all their hard work was in vain, Jesus majestically walked from the grave, He asked this question;

1 Corinthians 15:55, O death, where is your sting? O grave, where is your victory?

Matthew 28 v 1 – 6, v1, After the Sabbath, as the first day of the week began you dawn, Mary Magdalena and the other Mary came to see the tomb.

V2, and behold there was a great earthquake, for an angel of the Lord descended from heaven, and came and rolled back the stone from the door and ***sat on it,*** *V3 his countenance was like lightning and his clothing as white as snow.*

V4 and the guards shook for fear of him and became like dead men.

V5 but the angle answered and said to the women do not be afraid for I know that you seek Jesus who was crucified.

V6, He is not here, He is risen as He said, come see the place where the Lord lay.

The women worshipped the risen Jesus, *Matthew 28 v 9-10, and as they went to tell His disciples, behold, Jesus met them saying, rejoice, and they came and held Him by the and worshipped Him.*

V10, then Jesus said to them, do not be afraid, go and tell my brethren to go to Galilee and there will see me.

Jesus **finished** His work on earth, and went back to heaven, or I should say He went back home (heaven)

Acts 1v 9, now when He had spoken these things, while they watched, He was taken up and a cloud received Him out of their sight.

After He had spoken, what were Jesus' last words on earth?

Acts 1:8, but you shall receive power when the holy spirit has come upon you, and you shall be witnesses to me in Jerusalem and in all Judea and Samaria and to the end of the earth.

This is dear to Jesus, He *told* the disciples after His departure, as my Father sent me so I send you. (go and fish men, souls for me)

John 20:21, Then Jesus said to them again, " peace to you! As the Father sent me, I'm sending you,"

Jesus' yearning for souls, when He began to teach He talked the same language, preach the gospel. While studying my Bible I came across Jesus' words after John had been put to prison:

Jesus begins His ministry, *Mark 1:14-15, Now after John had been put to prison, Jesus came to Galilee, preaching the gospel of the Kingdom of God.*

V15, the time is fulfilled and the Kingdom of God is at hand, repent and believe in the gospel.

Mark 16: 15 and He said to them, " go into the whole world and preach the gospel to every creature.

Mark 16:16-18, v16, he who believes and is baptised will be saved, but he who does not believe will be condemned.

V17, and these signs shall follow them those who believe in my name, (signs shall follow soul winners) they shall cast out demons.

V18, they will speak with new tongues. They will take up serpents and if they drink anything deadly, it will by no means hurt them. They will lay hands on the sick and they will recover.

In Matthew 28:18-20, says, then Jesus came and spoke to them saying, all authority has been given to me in heaven and on earth.

V19, go therefore and make the disciples of all nations, baptising them in the name of the Father and the son and of the Holy spirit.

V20, teaching them to observe all things that I have commanded you and lo, I'm with you always, even to the end of the age, Amen

*Mark 16:19-20, so then after the Lord had spoken to them, He was received up into heaven and sat down at the right hand of God, a**nd they** went out and preached every where the Lord working with them and confirming the accompanying signs, Amen*

In the book of Romans Paul also said,

Romans 10: 14-15, How shall they call on Him in whom they have not believed? And how shall they believe in Him of whom they not heard? And how shall they hear without a preacher? And how shall they preach unless they are sent? As it is written, "How beautiful are the feet of those who preach the gospel of peace, who bring glad tidings of good things.

Jesus did not leave us alone, what a loving Father He is! We know that He will come again but in the time being Jesus decided to give us a helper (Holy spirit)

Mark 1:4, and being assembled together with them, He commanded them not depart from Jerusalem, but to wait for the promise of the Father.

John 14 v16, And I will pray to the Father and He will give you another helper (comforter) that He may abide with you forever.

Matthew 14:18, Jesus said, I will not leave you orphans, I will come to you.

Coming of the Holy spirit;

Acts 2:2-4, Now when the day of Pentecost had fully come, they were all with one in one place. Ad suddenly there came a sound from heaven, as of a rushing mighty wind and it filled the whole house where there were sitting. Then there appeared to them forked tongues, as of fire and one sat upon each of them. And there were all filled with the holy spirit and they began to speak with other tongues, as the spirit gave them utterance.

Jesus left but He is coming back, the bride groom, the Lamb is coming to take His bride (His church home) Are you ready, is your rob washed and ready, *Jesus'* heavenly airline is ready take off, please, every one be ready with your boarding pass.

Acts 1v 10, and while they looked towards heaven as He(Jesus) went up, two men stood by them in apparel.

V11, who also said, "men of Galilee, why do you stand gazing up into heaven? This same Jesus who was taken up into heaven from you, will so come in like manner as you saw Him go into heaven.

Yes Jesus will come as disciples saw Him go, it will not be long it soon and we see Him again. Jesus did say that He was going to prepare a place for us.

John 14:2-3, Jesus said, I'm my Father's house, are many mansions, if it were not so, I would have told you. I go to prepare a place for you.

V3 I go to prepare a place for you. I will come and receive you to myself, that where I'm, there you may be also.

He said it in *John 14:19, a little longer and the world will see me no more, but you will see me because I live, I live you will live also.*

John 14:1, Jesus, spoke and said, let not your heart be troubled.

John 14:27-28, He said, peace I leave with you, my peace I give you, my peace I give you not as the world gives, do I give to you. Let not your heart be troubled, neither let it be afraid.

V28, you have heard me say to you, I'm going away and coming back to you, if you love me you would rejoice because I said, I'm going to the Father, for my Father is greater than I

OK, Jesus, bye, bye, see you at your second coming. But even now I know you are with us you just chose be invisible for a reason because who can fight air? Who can question air, I can't touch you but you are Mighty in me, Mighty with us, Since you have empowered us with the Holy spirit, we will make you known to the world, **God with us.** Very, very soon the bride is going to meet the bride groom. Every bride, those who have walked that road know how sweet and glorious they wanted to look before appearing in front of the bridegroom! You wanted your groom to look at you and say wow! So, what about Jesus? What will be Jesus' reaction! How will it be! Oh what a glorious day!

Revelation 19:7-8, let us be glad and give Him glory for the marriage of the Lamb has come, and His wife has made herself ready.

V8, and to her it was granted to arrayed in fine linen, clean and bright, for the fine linen is the righteous act of the saints.

He is coming back for His bride, for a church without stain or wrinkle. Every woman knows how much time, effort and may be money we put out just to achieve that radiant spotless skin. And what is so funny is that we tent focus on the face but what about legs or arms? We spend time in front of the **mirror**, looking and checking. We even know how to hide those remaining spots with concealer, to make ourselves appear beautiful on the outside but inside is of full of blemishes! Hello!

Ephesians 5 v 25-27, v25, Husbands, love your wives just as Christ loved the Church and gave Himself up for her.

(26,that He might sanctify and cleanse it with the washing of water and the word,

27, He did this to present her to Himself as a radiant Church, without stain or wrinkle or any other blemish, but holy and blameless.

Colossians 1:22, but now He has reconciled you by Christ's physical body through death to present you holy in his sight, without blemish and free from accusations, NIV)

I sing my song:

I will sing all the praises for the one who died for me,
I will sing all the praises for the one who died for me.
I will give Him all the glory, He is worthy to be praised,
I will sing all the praises for the one who died for me.
Jesus is coming, Jesus is coming,
Jesus is coming, back for you and me,
Jesus is coming, back for you and me
End.

When? Very soon but when? It is soon and unexpectedly, like a thief in the night.

No one knows the day or hour!

Matthew 24 V 36, Jesus said, but of the day and hour no one knows, not even the angels of heaven buy the my Father only.

As it was in the day of Noah!

Matthew 24 V 37-38, but as the days of Noah were, so also will the coming of the Son of Man be.

V38, For in the days before of the flood, they were eating and drinking, marrying and giving in marriage until the day that Noah entered the ark.

Matthew 24 V 40-41, two men will be in the field, one will be taken and the other left, two women will be grinding at the mill, one will be taken and the other left.

Matthew 24 V42, watch therefore, you do not know what hour your Lord is coming.

V44, be ready, for the Son of Man is coming at an hour you do not expect Him.

1Thessalonians 5 V2,the day of the Lord, for you yourselves know perfectly that the day of the Lord so comes as a thief in the night.

1 Thessalonians 5:4, but you, brethren, you are not in the dark, so that this day should overtake as a thief.

When I was a child my grandfather (father's mother) used to sing a song, especially in the night, ***I'm so blessed I found Jesus, I'm so blessed I found Jesus.***

At that time I did not really understand my grandmother's song and I can't even remember if she was born gain or not but she loved such songs, ***I have decided to follow Jesus, I have decided to follow Jesus, no turning back, no turning back!*** The moment we heard *her* singing these songs then we knew that she was heading to sleep, and I can forget how we used to fight to keep her company! It was fun being with our grandmother because she knew how to spoil us with her food, let her *food* be as cold as freezer (two days) we will still eat it and leave our mother's even if fresh. Anyway this is not the point but.....!

1 Thessalonians 4 V 16-17, for the Lord Himself will descend from heaven with a shout, with the voice of an archangel, and with a trumpet of God and the dead in Christ will rise first.

V17, then we who are alive and remain shall be caught up together with them in cloud to meet the Lord in the air and thus we shall always be with the Lord.

Matthew 16 V 26-27, as Jesus spoke to His disciples said, for what profit is it to a man if he gains the whole world and loses his own soul? Or what will also man give in exchange for his soul?

V27, for the son of Man will come in the glory of His Father with His angels and then He will reward each according to his work.

1 Corinthians 15 V 51-52, behold, I tell you a mystery, we shall not all sleep but we shall all be changed.

V52, in a moment, in the twinkle of an eye, at the last trumpet, for the trumpet will sound and the dead will be raised incorruptible and we shall be changed.

Sometimes I wonder how it will be! In 2012, I found myself writing this song I did not know why it came to my spirit! **On the day I will see Jesus!**

On the day I will see Jesus, the humble King, who died for me,
On the day I will see Jesus, I will fall on my knees,
I will lay prostate before Him, I will praise Him, I will praise Him.
Jesus, I will praise you, on that day when I see you face to face,
Jesus, I will praise you, on that day when I see you!

I will praise you Jesus, on that day when I see you face to face,
Oh, that day, oh that day is coming, Oh, that day, oh that is coming,
Oh, that day is coming, it is coming, and it is coming soon!

Jesus will come, as His disciples saw Him going,
Jesus will come, as His disciples saw Him going,
He will come in His glory, He will come in His glory,
And those who believed in Him, and those who believed in Him,
Shall shout hallelujah, shall shout hallelujah
We are going home.
Shall shout hallelujah.
We are going home.

Sometimes I wonder, sometimes I wonder!
How it will be, to see the King of kings, face to face!
Sometimes I wonder, sometimes I wonder!
How it will be to see the King of kings, face to face!
Shake His hand, shake His hand.

Sometimes I wonder, sometimes I wonder!
How it will look like, to see the face of Jesus every day.
Sometimes I wonder, sometimes I wonder!
How it will look like to see the face of Jesus every day.
Oh, Jesus, Jesus, on that day, Jesus, I will bow on my knees
I will bow on my knees, eheeh, Jesus.

I really want to come where you are, Jesus,
I really want to come where you are, Jesus,
I really want come where you are, Jesus,
I really want to come Jesus,
I really want to come.
Precious Jesus, you are waiting for me
I really want to come were you are, Jesus,
On that day, I really want to see you face to face.

Wonderful Jesus, precious King of kings,
Wonderful Jesus, precious King of kings,
I will worship you, I will worship you.
I will worship you,
Your name, your name,
I will sing holy, holy, holy, holy,
I'm going home.
Holy, holy, I'm going home.
End.

Somewhere in this song it says, Jesus will come, and those who believed in Him shall shout hallelujah, we are going home. So I compered this with *John 3:36, whoever believes in the Son has eternal life, but whoever rejects the Son will not see life, for God's wrath remains in him.*

Jesus is too beautiful to be rejected, why should you perish when Jesus died on the cross for your sins? Jesus is looking forward to receiving you in heaven, *John 3:14-15, as Moses lifted the serpent in the wilderness, Jesus was also lifted up, that whoever believes in Him should not perish but have eternal life.*

Look to Jesus and be saved, believe in Him and escape condemnation.

John 3:18,he who believes in Him is not condemned, but he who does not condemned already because he has not believed in the name of the only begotten Son of God.

If you believe Jesus as your Lord and Saviour, you will have everlasting life. You will not be ashamed at His coming, say not to satan and receive the love of Jesus.

Romans 10:9, If you confess with your mouth the Lord Jesus and believe in your heart that God raised Him from the dead, you will be saved.

Romans 10:10, For with heart one believes to righteousness and with the mouth confession is made to salvation.

Prayer, Lord Jesus, I believe you died for me, I believe that God raised you from the dead. Please forgive me, I choose to turn away from my sins, I ask you to come into my heart and my life as my Lord and Saviour. I choose to serve you for the rest of my life. Amen.

Romans 10:13, Whoever calls upon the name of the Lord shall be saved.

Are you among Jesus' invited guests? Blessed are those who are called to the marriage supper of the Lamb. I conceived this song while reading *revelation 19:9, then he said to me, "write: Blessed are those who are called to the marriage supper of the Lamb!' " And he said to me, these are the true sayings of God.*

Sing with me this song:

Blessed are those who are called, to the marriage supper of the Lamb,
Blessed are those who are called, to the marriage supper of the Lamb.

Blessed are those, blessed are those, who are called,
To the marriage supper of the Lamb.
To the marriage supper of the Lamb.
To the marriage supper of the Lamb.
There will be no weeping.
There will no worries.
There will be no fighting.
Hallelujah, ohoo.

We will be singing.
We will be dancing.
We will be laughing.
Hallelujah, ohoo.

Blessed are those, blessed are those, who are called,
To the marriage supper of the Lamb.
To the marriage supper of the Lamb.
To the marriage supper of the Lamb.

We will be rejoicing!
We will be rejoicing!
What a wonderful time, in the presence of the Lord.
What a wonderful time in the presence of the Lord.
We will sing forever.
We will dance forever.
We will laugh forever.
Our God Almighty reigns.
Our God Almighty reigns.

Invitations are still on.
Invitations are still on.
You are invited, you are invited.
To the marriage supper of the Lamb.
To the marriage supper of the Lamb.
To the marriage supper of the Lamb.

Every body get ready, every body set- go.
Every body get ready, every body sea- go.
The table must be full.
The table must be full.
The table of Jesus- it must be full.
The table of Jesus- it must be full.

Every body get ready, every body set- go.
Every body get ready, every body set- go.
The Bridegroom is coming.
Jesus is coming.
Jesus is coming.
He is coming, He is coming and He is coming very, very soon!
He is coming, He is coming and He is coming very, very soon!
He has rewards in His hands, He has rewards in His hands.
To give to each and every one, according to what we have done.
To give to each and every one, according to what we have done.

Every body get ready, every body set-go
Every body get ready, every body set-go.
Are you among His invited guests? Are you among His invited guests?
To the marriage supper of the Lamb.
To the marriage supper of the Lamb.
To the marriage supper of the Lamb.
His table must be full.
His table must be full.
The table of Jesus- it must be full.
The table of Jesus- it must be full.

Yes, I am among His invited guests, yes, I am among His invited guests.
To the marriage supper of the Lamb.
To the marriage supper of the Lamb.
To the marriage supper of the Lamb.

We are going, we are going, to meet our Bridegroom in air.
We are going, we are going, to meet our Bridegroom in air.
You are coming, you are coming, to meet the Bridegroom in air.
You are coming, you are coming, to meet the Bridegroom in air.
We shall shout hallelujah, we shall shout hallelujah.
Our Bridegroom has com.
We shall shout hallelujah, we shout hallelujah.
Our Bridegroom has come.

Hell must emptied, hell must be emptied.
We will all go, we will all go.
To the marriage supper of the Lamb.
To the marriage supper of the Lamb.

No one must be left behind.
No one must be left behind.
We will all go, we will all go.
To the marriage supper of the Lamb.
To the marriage supper of the Lamb.
To the marriage supper of the Lamb.

The table must be full.
The table must be full.
The table of Jesus- it must be full.
Blessed- are- those, blessed- are- those, who are called.
To the marriage supper of the Lamb.
To the marriage supper of the Lamb.
To the marriage supper of the Lamb.
Amen.
End.

Reading the book of revelation my God given song keeps coming alive in me.

Revelation 21:1-8, And I saw a new heaven and new earth, for the first heaven and the first earth had passed away, also there was no more sea.

V2, The I John saw the holy city, new Jerusalem coming down out of heaven from God, prepared as a bride adorned for her husband.

V3, And I heard a loud voice from heaven saying, behold, the tabernacle of God is with men and He will dwell with and they shall be His people and God Himself will be with them and be their God.

V4, and God will wipe away every tear from our eyes: there shall be no more death, nor sorrow, nor crying: and there will be no more pain, for the former things have passed away.

V5, Then He said, I make all things new," And He said to me, "write, for these words are true and faithful.

V6, and He said to me, "It is done! " I am the Alpha and Omega, the Beginning and the End. I will give the fountain of water of life freely to him who is thirsts.

V7, he who overcomes shall inherit all things and I will be his God and he shall be my son.

V8, but the cowardly, unbelieving, murderers, sexual immoral, sorcerers, idolaters, and shall have their part in the lake which burns with fire and brimstone, which is the second death.

In the above song somewhere it says, Jesus is coming very soon. He has rewards in His hand to give to each and every one according to what we have done.

Revelation 22:7, behold I'm coming quickly! Blessed is he who keeps the words of the prophecy of this book.

Revelation 22:12, and behold, I'm coming quickly and my reward is with me, to give to everyone according to his work.

Saints reign with Christ!

Revelation 20: 6, *Blessed and holy is he who has part in the first resurrection, over such the second death has no power but they shall be priests of God and of Christ. And shall reign with Him a thousand years.*

Going back to *revelation 20:12, and I saw the dead, small and great, standing before God, and books were opened and another book was opened which is the book of life. And dead were judged according to their works by the things which were written in the books.*

Revelation 20:15, and any one whose name was not found written in the book of life was thrown into the lake of fire. (NIV)

NKJV, and any one not found written in the book of life was cast into the lake of fire.

Heaven is beautiful, it is worth fighting for, and place where you will not need to pay electric bills, or need any sun shine!

Revelation 21:23, the city no need of sun or of the moon to shine in it, for the glory of God illuminates it. The Lamb is it's light.

Think about everything in heaven:

Think about everything in heaven, think about everything in heaven.
Jesus has everything for you, in heaven.
Jesus has everything for you, in heaven.

A place where you will never angry, in heaven.
A place where you will never be depressed, in heaven.
A place where you will never be worried, in heaven.
A place where you will never hungry, in heaven.
A place where you will never be thirsty, in heaven.
A place where you will never grow old, in heaven.
A place where you will want have to walk on the streets of gold, in heaven.
Jesus has everything for you, in heaven.
Jesus has everything for you, in heaven

It doesn't matter what you are going through right now.
Lift your eyes and look, in heaven.
Lift your eyes and look, in heaven.
Jesus has everything for you, in heaven.
Jesus has everything for you, in heaven.

Angels will your waiters, in heaven.
You will be eating with Jesus, in heaven.
Jesus has everything for you, in heaven.
Jesus has everything for you, in heaven.
You never wish to put shoes, in heaven.
Jesus has everything for you, in heaven.
Jesus has everything for you, heaven.
End.

God said, I believe it, I believe what I'm reading from this holy Book, if heaven is as beautiful and peaceful as John the revelatory described then it worth fighting for! Who would not love to walk on pure gold as transparent as glass?

John testified in *revelation 21:21(B), And I saw the city was pure gold, like transparent glass.*

Revelation 21:22, but I saw no temple in it, for the Lord Almighty is and the Lamb are it's temple.

I bring the book of Isaiah here, God the glory of His people;

Isaiah 60:19-20, The sun shall not longer be your light by day, nor for brightness shall the moon give light to you. But the Lord will be to you an everlasting light and your God your glory. Your sun shall no longer go down, nor your moon withdraw itself: for the Lord will be your everlasting light.

But the tribe of those who are saved, the born again ones are the ones who will walk in it.

Revelation 21:24-25, and the nations of those who are saved shall walk in its light and the kings of the earth brings their honour into it. Its gates shall not shut at all by day, there shall be no light there. (we are kings) Going back John Jesus' conversation with Nicodemus:

John 3:3, Jesus answered him (Nicodemus), "most assuredly, I say to you, unless one is born again, he cannot see the Kingdom of God."

V4, Nicodemus asked Jesus, "how can a man be born when he is old? Can help enter a second time into his mother's womb and be born?

V5, Jesus answered, "most assuredly, I say you, unless one is born of water and the spirit, he cannot enter the Kingdom of God.

V7, Jesus said, do not marvel that I said to you, you must be born again.

V14-15, and as Moses lifted up the serpent in the wilderness, even so must the son of Man be lifted up that whoever believes in Him should not perish but have eternal life.

Now coming back to the revelation of John:

Revelation 21:18-19, and the constrictions of its walls was Jasper and the city was of pure gold, like clear glass. And the foundations of the wall of the city were adorned with all kinds of precious stones, the first foundation was jasper, the second sapphire......!

I tell you, you will it there!

Revelation 21:21, And the twelve gates were twelve pearls: each individual gate was one pearl. And the streets of the city was pure gold, like transparent glass.

Then, *in revelation 21:27, but there shall by no means* ***enter into it*** *anything that defiles or causes abomination or a lie but only those whose are written in the Lamb's book of life.*

The angle who spoke to John showed him, *a* pure river *of* the water of life,

Revelation 22:1, And he showed me a pure river of the water of life, clear as crystal proceeding from the throne of God and of the Lamb.

Revelation 22: 2, In the middle of its Street and either side of the river was the tree of life which bore twelve fruits, each tree yielding its fruit every month and the leaves of the tree were for the healing of the nations.

And there shall be no more curse but the throne of God and the Lamb shall be in it. And His servants shall serve Him, revelation 22:3.

We will see Jesus' face and His name will be on our foreheads.

Revelation 22:4, They shall see His face and His name shall be on their foreheads!

Think about everything, in heaven, Jesus has everything for you in heaven!

Revelation 22:5, there shall be no ***night*** *there, they need no lump nor light of the sun, for the Lord God gives them light and they shall reign for ever and ever.*

(No nights there, we will never be in need of lump or lights, for the Lord God will give us light and we shall reign for ever and ever, with Him. How beautiful!

Revelation 22:13-15, I am the Alpha and the Omega, the Beginning and End, the First and the Last. Blessed are those who do His commandments that they may have the right to the tree of life and may enter through the gate into the city. But outside are dogs and sorcerers and sexually Immoral and murderers and idolaters and whoever loves and practises a lie.

Revelation 22:16, I, Jesus, has sent my angel to testify to you these things, in the churches. Iam the Root and the offspring of David, the Bright and the Morning Star.

Revelation 22:17, And the spirit and the Bride say, "Come, let him who hears say, "Come, And let him who thirsts come and whoever desires , let take the water of life freely

Revelation 22:6, Then he said to me, these words are faithful and true," and the Lord God of the holy prophets sent His angle His servants the things which must shortly take place.

Singing this song, Jesus has everything for you in heaven, I was actually comforting myself and telling **Betty,** myself that I didn't / does not matter any situation, Jesus has everything for me in heaven. Lift you eyes and look in heaven, Jesus has everything for me in heaven, it doesn't what you are going through right now.

1 corinthians 2:9, Eye has not seen, nor ear heard, nor have entered the heart of man, things which God has prepared for those who love Him.

So why did Jesus had to leave such a beautiful place, heaven where Streets are made of gold to come and walk on dust for thirty three years? He wore sandals even His tomb was borrowed. Jesus lived like a poor Man. There is a common verse in the Bible, He became poor to make me rich.

2 corinthians 8:9, For I, know the grace of our Lord Jesus Christ, that though He was rich, yet for my sake He became poor, that through His poverty I might become rich.

Because of love Jesus came into this world, He left His heavenly glory and lived among us. He laid all the splendours of heaven down and humbled Himself to be like us in all things. Born of a virgin girl, He was born and grew up just like us.

Luke 1: 30-31, then the angle said to her, "do not be afraid, Mary, for you have found favour with God.

V31, and behold, you shall conceive in your womb and bring forth a son, and you call His name Jesus.

Jesus became tired, *John 4:6, now Jacob's well was there, Jesus therefore being wearied from His journey sat by the well. It was about the sixth hour.*

Jesus was hungry, *Mark 11:12, when they had come out from Bethany, He was hungry.*

Jesus slept, *Matthew 8:24, and suddenly, a great tempest arose on the sea, so that the boat was covered with waves. But He was asleep.*

Jesus was accused, *Matthew 27:12, and while He was being accused by the chief priests and the elders, He answered nothing.*

Jesus wrote on the sand, *John 8:6, but Jesus stooped down and wrote on the ground with His finger as though He did not hear.*

Jesus wept, John 11:35.

Jesus became angry! *Matthew 21:12-13, then Jesus went into the temple of God and drove out all who bought and sold in the temple and overturned the tables of money changers and the seats of those who sold doves.*

V13, and He said to them, it is written, my house shall be called a house of prayer, but you have made a den of thieves.

Mark 3:5, so when He had looked around at them with anger, being grieved at by the hardness of their hearts, He said to the man, stretch out your hand. And He stretched it out and his hand was restored as whole as the other.

Jesus was tempted, *Matthew 4:3-4, now the temper came to Jesus and said to Him, if you are the Son of God, command that these stones become bread.*

V4, but He answered and said, it is written, Man shall not live by bread alone but every word that proceeds from the mouth of God.

Jesus prayed: *Luke 6:12, now it came to pass in those days that Jesus went to the mountain to pray, and He continued all night in prayer to God.*

Mark 1:35, now in the morning having risen a long while before daylight Jesus went out and departed to solitary place and there He prayed.

Matthew 14:23, and when He had sent the multitudes away, He went up on a mountain by Himself to pray. And evening had come He was alone there.

Jesus fasted : *Matthew 4:2, and when he had fasted fourty days and fourty nights, afterwards He was hungry.*

Jesus attended a wedding: *John 2:1-3, On the third day there was a wedding in Cana Galilee and the mother of Jesus was there.*

V2, now both Jesus and His disciples were invited, to the wedding. V3, and when they had ran out of wine, the mother of Jesus said to Him, they had no wine.

Jesus sweat: *Luke 22:44, and being in agony, He played more earnestly and His sweat became like great drops of blood falling to the ground.*

Jesus was betrayed by a friend: *Luke 22:48, but Jesus said to him, Judas, are you betraying the Man with a kiss?*

Luke 22:21, but behold, the hand of my betrayer is with me on the table.

Even someone denied Jesus: *Luke 22 : 56-57,* ***Peter denied Jesus****, and a servant girl seeing him as he sat by the fire, looked intently at him and said, this man was also with Him (Jesus) but* ***he*** *denied Him saying, woman, I don't Him!*

Luke 22:58, after a little while another saw him and said, you are one of them, but Peter said, man, I am not!

Luke 59-60, then after an hour had passed, another confidently affirmed, saying," surely this fellow also was with them, for he is a Galilean, but Peter said, " man I don't know what you are saying!

Jesus was arrested: *Luke 22:1, then having arrested Him they led Him and brought Him into the high priest's house and Peter followed at a distance.*

Jesus was also beaten: *Mark 15:19, then they struck Him on the head with a reed and spat on Him.*

Jesus was mocked: *and when they had mocked Him, they took the purple off Him, put His own clothes on Him and led Him out to crucify Him.*

Jesus kept silence: *Mark 15:4-5, then Pilate asked Him again, do you answer nothing see how many things they testify against you? But Jesus still answered nothing, so that Pilate marvelled.*

Jesus also became thirsty: *John 19:28, after this Jesus knowing that all things were now accomplished, that scriptures might be fulfilled, said, I, thirsty!*

John 4 :7, a woman of Samaria came to draw water, Jesus said to her, "give me a drink!"

Jesus rode on a donkey: *Mark 11:77-8, then they brought a colt to Jesus and they threw their garments on it and He sat on it. And many spread their garments on the road and others cut down leafy branches from the trees and spread them on the road.*

They laughed at Jesus: *Luke 8 : 53-55, and they laughed at Him to scorn, knowing that she was dead. But He put them all out, took her by the hand and called, saying, little girl arise. Then her spirit returned and she arose immediately.*

Jesus **died:** *John 19 :30, so when Jesus had received the soar wine, He said, "it is finished!" And bowing His head He gave up His spirit.*

Jesus was **buried**: *John 19 :38, then they took the body of Jesus, and bound it in stripes of linen with the spices as the custom of Jews in burying.*

John 19:42, So there they laid Jesus because of the Jews' preparation day, for the tomb was nearby.

Jesus observed social distance, as I was in my kitchen washing my dishes while writing my book in my book, I thought about some verses in the Bible where it says, that withdrew Himself a distance from His disciples. So I said, yes, Jesus also observed social distance!

Luke 22:41, And Jesus was withdrawn from them about a stone's throw and He knelt down and prayed.

Mark 14:35, Jesus went a little further and fell on the ground and prayed that it were possible the hour might pass from Him.

Matthew 26:29, Jesus went a little further and fell on His face and prayed saying, oh, my father if it is possible, let this cup pass from me, nevertheless not as I will but as you will.

But thought Jesus died like any other man He to life after three days: *Matthew 27:5-6, but the angle answered and said to the women, do not be afraid, for I know that you seek Jesus who was crucified. 6, He is not here, He is risen as He said, come and see the place where the Lord lay.*

Jesus' disciples were in a **lock down:** *John 20:19, then, the same day evening being the first day of the week, when the doors were shut where the disciples were assembled for fear of the Jews.* ***Jesus came and stood in the midst and said to them, peace be with you.***

John 20:26,and after eight days Jesus' disciples were again inside, and Thomas with them Jesus came, the doors being shut and stood in the midst and said, peace to you.

So Jesus is saying **again**, peace, let there be calm! *John 20:21, then Jesus said it again, peace to you!*

Jesus' disciples still in lock down until Pentecost Sunday as we were!

Acts 1:4-5, and being assembled together with them, He commanded them not to depart from Jerusalem but to wait for the promise of the Father. 5, for truly John baptized with water but you shall be baptized with Holy Spirit on many days from now.

Coming of the Holy Spirit: *Acts 2:1-4, now when the days of the Pentecost had fully come, they were all with one accord in one place.*

2, and suddenly there came a sound from heaven as are rushing mighty wind, and it filled the whole house where there were sitting.

3, then there appeared to them forked tongues as of fire and one sat upon each of them.

4, and they were all, filled with the Holy Spirit and began to speak with other tongues as the Spirit gave them utterance.

During lock down I experienced these type of wind twice in my bedroom!

Saturday morning 30th May/ 2020, still in lock down, that early morning I woke up to worship and praised God. I spent much time in my living room worshipping because for some reason I had dedicated the month of May just to worship and to give Him thanks. Though I had decided just to worship, it is a must that I should pray our Lord's prayer! And other psalms like psalm 23 and psalm 91. After I, had worshipped God, I read my Bible as usual. But that Saturday morning since I knew that my Pastor was not coming live with us (morning glow) I decided to sleep again. As I was in deep sleep. I had this dream but it looked as real. There was too much wind in my bedroom, the wind blew to the extent that I could feel curtains in my window being swamped. My bedroom was shaking, I felt so cold as if I was standing outside. I began to shiver as I was shivering I was talking, saying Jesus, Jesus, for many times! I tried had to get up because I wanted to see if my son was awake. In that dream I wanted to tell him to stay in his bedroom because I thought the wind might swipe him, but I couldn't. In my heart I was saying I hope Isaiah is not awake at this time. Still shouting, Jesus, Jesus, from nowhere I saw this ugly black thing, but it looked like a suit case, it was as ugly as it could be! As I looked at it and wondering where it came from? Or who could have put such an ugly thing on my bed, the wind swamped it. Then it seized and whole bedroom was calm. Then as I looked again, someone who I cannot explain came and brought this beautiful white sheet and spread it on top of my bed. I can't call it a bed cover or a bedsheet but it covered my entire bed. OK, in my heart I could see that person and I could see a hand spreading that sheet on my bed but my natural eyes couldn't recognise him fully. After spreading that white sheet on my bed he left.

Then on Saturday again 29th June I had the same experience, always after my early morning worship routine! Trying to figure out what it could it be! But this time after I had been fully and done with dreaming I jumped from my bed and opened my curtain to see outside because in a dream it felt as if I was day time. I thought I could see what I saw in a dream but! That morning again after I had worshipped, prayed and read the Bible, I slept in my sleep I felt too much wind blowing in my bedroom. I felt very cold and in that dream it was raining in my very bedroom, because I was trying cover myself. I wondered why there was too much wind then I looked out side and I saw a woman, she was behind our house but living in a shade, she had four children. Something told me, you need to and bring that woman and her children in the house, but in heart I was saying where will I put her and the children because I looked as if my son and I were sharing on bedrooms. I did not remember that my son had his own bedroom so I said to whoever was sending me to pick a homeless woman and her children from the shade, I will do it next time. But the person insisted, go and bring them now! So I went, intending to share my bedroom with her, her children and my son. I went, when I reached I asked her, have you told housing that you need a house? She said yes, but they were unable to help her. I saw a man far from her but I did not speak to him, I told her that I was there to pick her and her children, she quickly handed me her baby so I brought them to my house₩ then I was saying now I will not do the things I'm used to do because I will be looking after this woman and her children! As we were busy unpacking her luggage I woke up. Waking up from sleep, I said, I thought it was raining! Recovering from the dream I got up from the bed, opened my curtains, I looked behind my house to see if I could see any woman with children but I did not see anyone! I said, is there any woman somewhere who needs help? I kept on looking to see if I could see a homeless woman with children, and that woman I dreamt happened to be a smoker! Thought that is why I was reluctant. On Monday my son and I went out, but I was looking around on the street to see if there was a homeless woman. When were coming back I saw a woman sitting the super market and asking money from people but she did not have any children, I stopped and greeted her, then I asked, do you have need any food? Likely we had bought ripe bananas, I handed those bananas to her and she ate. I asked her, where do you live? She answered, everywhere really! She was homeless but not with children. I'm yet to understand why all those winds blew in bedroom during lock down!

Jesus Light of the world

Light of the world, Jesus is the **way** and He is **light**, light of the world, Light to my pass, *Psalm 119:105,says, your word is a lamp to my feet and a light to path.*

James 1:17, Every good gift and every perfect gift is from above and comes down from the Father of light, with whom there is not shadow of turning.

John 8 v12,*Then Jesus said I'm the light of the world whoever follows me will not walk in darkness but have the light of life.*

John 12:26, While you have light, believe in the light that that you may become sons of light. These things Jesus spoke and departed and was hidden from them.

Acts 9:3, And he journeyed, he came near Damascus, and suddenly, a light shone around him from.

Acts 13:47, For the Lord commanded us, I have set you to be a light to the Gentles that you should bring salvation to the end of the earth.

Daniel 2:22, He reveals deep and secret things, He knows what is in the darkness and light dwells with Him.

Psalm 36:9, For with you, God is the fountain of life, in your we see light.

Way, light! He is the way if you walk in Him or follow Him you can never be lost. He is the straight path and there are no corners or short cuts in Jesus. follow the straight path and you will reach your destination. We have known that Jesus is the light of the world, so how can you follow light and be lost?

John 12:35, Jesus said to them, "walk while you have the light lest darkness overtakes you, he who walks in darkness does not know where he is going. Why choose darkness when there is light?

Matthew 4:26, the people who sat in darkness have seen the great light and upon those who sat in the region and shadow of death light has dawned.

John 12:46, I have come, as light into the world that whoever believes in me should not abide in darkness.

It is those who walk in darkness or follow darkness that get lost because they are not able to see where are going. When you are in dark the only thing you see is darkness. You can't follow Jesus and end in hell fire, no way! Supposing you are walking in the night and it's very dark will you be able to see the pit that is front of you if you have no light? Of course not! If you cannot see it what happens next, is to fall inside that pit but when you have the light you will be able to recognise that there is a pit a head of you.

Light will make you avoid that pit, light is very beautiful it also exposes those things that are in darkness.

John 1:4-5, In Him was life and the life was the light of men, and Light shines in the darkness and the darkness has not overcome it.

Genesis 1:3, And God said, let there be light," and there was light.

Psalm 18:28, For you will light my lamp, the Lord my God will enlighten my darkness.

Luke 2:32, And light to bring revelation to the Gentile and the glory of your people Israel.

Psalm 80:18, Restore O Lord God of host, cause your face to shine and we shall be saved.

Living a life without Jesus, is living in darkness. if we follow Jesus, (light) we will not fall into that pit, hell. When my mother was alive she had a song:

Follow, follow I will follow Jesus,
anywhere, everywhere I will follow Him,
follow, follow I will follow Jesus,
every where He leads me I will follow Him.
End.

One Sunday, early 2018, I dressed my son for church, I think looking in the mirror he liked his suit through that happiness he wrote a song! I follow Jesus, what did Jesus had to do with his new suit?

My son's song: I follow Jesus, I follow Jesus
Yes, I do, yes, I do.
I, follow Jesus, I follow Jesus,
Yes, I do, yes I do.
He is the way, the truth and life.

I, follow Jesus, I follow Jesus, I follow Jesus.
Yes, I do.
End.

You have to make up your mind to follow Jesus, in Him life is guarantee **I said, why suffer if love is able to help me?**

I can remember after I had decided to follow Jesus ***again*** in 2011, some how I despaired, within me I, knew I was born again though I did not know how to maintain my walk with Him. I could have thought that Jesus would automatically take all my challenges at once. I remember one day during Bible study we were asked a question one by one, why did you come to Jesus? We all had answers and reasons and I'm sure many people who have come to Jesus were drawn by different facts. But above all it's because of love and running away from that path which leads someone to hell fire. Deep down In me I knew thought I love Jesus, I said yes to Him because I had many challenges and that Sunday's message matched with what I was going through. So I said why suffer? Let me go to Jesus if He is able to solve this hard life. What I know for sure, is, devil was not happy losing me, but I was determined.

New and young in the Lord I woke up one morning singing praise and worshipping, then something came to mind. I did not know how to explain this Jesus according to how I was feeling at that moment. I was so happy like I had never been,before, as I sang praises I just gave Him a name, I don't know if it made sense to others but it made sense to me! I called Jesus the *impossible doer!* It's true because Angle Gabriel told Mary in *Luke 1:37, For with God nothing shall be impossible.* Thought we speak and say that there is nothing our God cannot do, to me, there something He cannot do, *He cannot lie*! Nothing is too hard for Jesus. If you need solution for that which you are looking to solve, the answer is at your door. Jesus is at your door and His is knocking (the door of your heart) Open for Him and let Him enter. Let Him give you solution to that problem. It might be hard for man but not with God.

I received a song in 2012, **He is knocking:**

Jesus is standing at the door, He is knocking,
will you let Him come? Will you let Him come in?
He wants to dine with you, He wants to dine with you.
Jesus wants to dine with you, He wants to dine with you.
Will you let Him come in?
End.

God loves His children so much! In most cases when people have something to discuss, they arrange a meeting, invite each other and have dinner together. Sitting together at that dinner table makes it easier to discuss and come up with solutions. Then what about Jesus, the Most High God, standing at your door, He wants to give you a solution to that problem that has been troubling you. Are you going to open your heart for Jesus? You better let Jesus in, have dinner with Him and talk about business. You cannot have dinner with Jesus and remain the same! Tell Jesus everything you are going through, He is the only answer. The Bible says:

Behold, I stand at the door and I, knock, if anyone hears my voice and opens the door I will come in to him and dine with him and he with me, Revelation 3:20.

I was at my friend's house, as I was on the computer, typing and singing this song came to my mouth: *If you are tired and needs rest, I know someone who is so kind, just come to Him, He will take care of you and give you rest.*

Jesus loves you and His mercy endless. Are you heavy burdened and thinking that there is no body to help you? There is a saviour Jesus Christ, His love is for everyone come to Him and you will find peace,

Matthew 11:28, *come to me all you who are weary and burdened and I will give you rest.*

You can tell your friends, you can tell your family because we all need people to talk to, but none is like Jesus! Tell Him all your troubles and let Him be the solution, tell

Him all your hard problems and He will give you the answer. A friend and a saviour who will love you and save you. Jesus is the only one I know, call Him, He will hear, He will answer you. When Jesus says, I'm at your door, don't think He means the door if your house. Though it is a beautiful idea to let Him be ruler in your **house.** Jesus wants to touch you, He is looking to come into your heart, is there any space for Him? Remember He is bigger than the **universe** but gentle enough to live in you. This world may want to distrust us but if we hold on to Jesus, we will overcome it. This life is not a bed of roses, we face challenges. Storms of life will come but they cannot blow us if Master Jesus is with us. If we have Jesus in our boats we will sleep like babies. Having Jesus means standing firm, having Him is standing on the sold rock because when you are standing on that sold rock nothing can move you, you are immovable.

Psalm 62 v2, God is my rock and my salvation, He is my defence, I shall not be greatly moved.

Checking what it means to be immovable, I found out that immovable objects have graffiti sprayed on. Thought we are not objects! *Synonyms: fixed,* secure, stable, rooted, firm and so forth. Situations will try but in Jesus you will remain unshakeable.

Psalm 16:8, I have set the Lord always before me because He is at my right hand I shall not be moved.

It's good to trust in God and in His promises, He promised that He will never leave us nor forsake us,

Deuteronomy 31:8, And the Lord, He is the one goes before you, He will be with you, He will not leave you nor forsake you, do not fear nor be dismayed.

My song: *Jesus, you will never forsake me. Jesus, you will never leave me,*
Jesus will never leave me,
I'm standing on the promises, on the promises of Jesus.
I'm counting every good promise, that He promised me,
because I know He will never to me, I'm standing on the word of Jesus.
Yes I'm standing on the word of Jesus, the word of Jesus is my sold rock,

I will never be forsaken, Jesus will never forsake me.
Jesus, you are my hiding place, you are my hiding place,
My Refuge, My Tower.
When I call on Jesus, let me tell you He will answer me,
He will answer me, I know, He will answer me.
Jesus, has promised never to leave me, He has promised never to leave me.
Even though the wind wants to blow,
I know where to go, I know Jesus will, Jesus will hid me,
He will calm the wind for me, Jesus, you are my hiding place,
He said put your trust in me, He has promised, never to leave me.
Jesus, I will put my trust in you.
End.

I can have peace of mind even in the midst of challenges ***if I want!***

Philippians 4:7, And the peace of God which surpassed all understanding will guard your hearts and your minds in Christ Jesus.

OK, there are times when I feel like the world had ran away from me, but within me I still hear that still voice of comfort tells me, it is well! I know that there is something to worry about, but then I just choose to ignore. But here in a new me, and not the old me! Who would tell the old me not worry when I knew that needs were not met?!

In Philippians 4:6, do not be anxious, worry about anything but in everything by prayer and supplication with thanksgiving let your request be known to God.

I think someone can be happy and still be at peace in the midst of circumstances if you choose (I choose) to remove eyes from worldly troubles, because no matter how much you run we can't catch the world. In Jesus we can be at peace even if we don't have peace, if we hand over to Jesus,

John 16:33, Jesus said, these things I have spoken to you that in me you may have peace, in this world you will have tribulations but be of good cheer, I have overcome the world.

1 Peter 5 v7, casting all your cares upon Him, first He cares for you.

can be happy even if I'm not happy no matter what! In those I used to see my mother singing, and knowing how she was suffering, then I would wonder how and where she gets strength to sing and to be happy? She was joyful, rejoicing all the time!

I can now say my mother was living in *Philippians 4 v4, rejoice in the Lord, again I, will say rejoice. Nehemiah 8:10, the joy of the Lord is my strength,*

I one morning went to shop to buy some things, and this man just looked tired. As I tried to speak to Him he said, man!, I'm so stressed! Why? Business is not easy! I can't sleep at night man! I go home late and come out early! He took his time to explain to me what stresses him. So what is a difference? Really it's true that you can have all the money in world and still be depressed and empty because there is that place in your heart where Jesus only can fill but it is empty! Or I can say that there is something missing in you! would love to be that person who praises God even when things are not going well inseated of mourning around Him! I admit that there were/are times when I feel like there is no strength to praise God, because some things are missing in my life. So what if I just get up and start praising Him in that situation? Can feelings now decide for me or tell me not to praise God! It does not matter how you feel, good or bad God will always be God. In every situation He wants us to give Him glory! I, remember those days when I could not have food to eat, being homeless for good two weeks, walking on the road as if I was an inspector. On the streets of London! In the year 2005, what I did was to sleep on my stomach to get strength or make my belt too tight. Or I wish at that time I knew how to praise God. There is a song that says:

count your blessings and name them one by one and it will surprise you what the Lord has done!

If I can count my blessings then I know how to count! OK, I can start but can I really finish! I know some people, when you look at them, you can automatically see that this one must have one question for God, but then they are the most thankful! When it comes to praise God, you can't go near them! If could count how much breath I pour out every day then missing one meal a day couldn't stop me from praising God. So my friend, do not wait until you become a millionaire before you can start to glorify God. What is the best time to serve/ praise God? Is it in plenty or in hunger/ in need? It remains a question!

Joel 3:10, let the weak say I'm strong, let the poor say I'm rich.

I, may not be rich now but I'm alive to have hope, I'm alive to dream. OK, I may not have that car yet but I have legs to walk. I used to wonder, how can someone praise God in difficult times! I was like, if I praise God in times of trials, what am I, really thanking Him for? *But* the dead can never understand if there is a need or not and the dead cannot praise God so if you ask me now, I can tell you that I finally join the club of those who praise God in difficult times. I call it praising God any how. Praising Him to get something? Or thanking Him to receive something? All you have to do is, say thank you Jesus even if you haven't seen anything yet. If my son comes to me and says, mum, thank you my shoes and everyday he does the same. He hasn't seen the shoes yet! I will feel uncomfortable because how can someone keep thanking me for shoes that I haven't bought! To avoid that I will make sure that I buy that pair of shoes. God will not feel uncomfortable if you keep praising Him and thanking Him for what you have not seen, He will be moved to do it. I remember those days that I was thanking God for my two bedroom house, I knew I was not qualified to have because at that time I, did not have all the requirements that they needed, but as I praised Him day by day I did not know when I received! It was like a dream! Praises can soften hard situation, it's like soaking saucepan over night after cooking cornmeal, maize! Can someone praise God for who He is? Can someone give thanks to God for who He is? To me, I said, let me just thank Him for being God. Worshipping I don't worship God for what He has given me, I worship Him for being God. I think God feels more excited when He hears us adoring Him, just calling Him beautiful names, exalting Him for who He is. When I'm writing, with no intention of worship, I just find out that I'm worshipping God in praises, and then I wonder! I did not mean to praise, my intention was just worship, so how did I get into praises?! Sometimes I just write without even knowing what I'm writing, especially when I'm angry! Yes angry but laughing at situations, when situations try to tell me lies, expand themselves on me. So to me, writing that song, I'm actually abusing that devil and magnifying God, **who said I will not worship you?**

who said I will not worship you? Who said I will not worship you?
Who said I will not worship you? He's a liar, he's a liar, he's a liar, he's a liar!
I will worship you, Jesus, I will worship you, Jesus,
I will worship you, Jesus, I will bow on my knees and worship you,
I will bow on my knees and worship you, I will bow on my knees and worship you.
You are an Amazing God, you are an Amazing God,
I will worship you, I will worship you.
End.

This is what I did not know but since I discovered, it has made sense to me. If God was not God, would He have given me those things which I'm thanking Him for? I think worship goes before thanksgiving. If I acknowledge that God is God, then I would be able to know that I'm praise Him for the things He has done, because of who is He is! If I, can't worship, then praise will be far from me, because who am l praising in the first place? I wrote a song praising God for His power, greatness, honour and glory. Because God's power is just too mighty, I have seen His power:

Because of your majesty, because of your greatness.
Because of your power, honour and glory.
I will praise you King of kings, I will praise you Lord of lords
I will bow on my knees and worship you. Ehe Majesty I exalt you!
Majesty, I exalt you! I bow before your throne.
I bow at your feet.
Beautiful morning star, sweet Jesus ancient of days.
For there is none like you, Jesus, there is none like you!
Hassan in the highest, Hassan King of King.
Master of universe, Creator of all things
End.

As I kept on writing I saw that I was praising God for His Majesty or praising His Majesty. I can't say that it was a mistake because in my spirit that is how I felt! It was a short song but it carried too much volume:

oh Majesty, I want to praise you Jesus.
For who you are, for who you are King of kings.

For who you are, for you are Lord of Lords.
Majesty, I want to praise your name.
End.

I was at work as some of us sat in the staff room to have lunch, after eating my lunch I said, thank you Jesus for providing! Then another stubborn colleague asked me, who cooked food? I said it's me, then she said, thank yourself because God did not cook! I said OK then, but who gave me strength too cook,? Or who provided it? In my heart I said, I know you are looking for me but I will leave you with one word. I said, I'm nothing without Him! I could have kept quiet but there were other people in the room so I decided to tell everyone as if I was I was telling one person! In case someone wanted to hear it! When you bless food they look at you in a funny way as if you have committed that big crime! They look at each other and wink their eyes. Any time is a good time to say something good about Jesus. How can my mouth be idle when I know that I have something good to talk about God? It all started because I gave thanks to God for providing food.

Love is sharing, share Jesus' love with others

Talk about Jesus, tell others what you know about Jesus, you never if you could win them for Him! How will those who don't know Jesus come to know Him if we keep quiet? Since love is sharing then we need to share this *love.* They are people out there who do not know Jesus and they need someone to talk to them. Example when I was still living in a charity shared accommodation, I had someone who I called my friend. I did not know him but whenever I saw him I would I describe him as my friend! I think he lived near me because I used to see him each time I went out to a corner shop near nearby. He liked his drink, alcohol each time I saw him he was drank but I did not like seeing him in that state. Whenever I saw him I would feel sorry for him! So one day I decided to give him a leaflet, a track, I was looking for an opportunity tell him about Jesus. The first time I tried he was too drank, the second time he was also drank but I was determined. I tried to put that leaflet in his hand but he couldn't hold it because his hands were shaking! Finally I gave it to him and he put it in his pocket but said to him, "don't read it now, read it tomorrow morning. I wanted him to read about Jesus. One day again it happened that I saw him when he was still sober, he recognised me and smiled. I did not know why we were meeting all the time, but it happened that one day I saw him in the morning, he was with his cousin (teenager) he was still OK, again I talked to him about God but inseated he said to me, "I want to go out with you! I answered him, I also want you to give up this drinking! Then he asked me, "but why are so kind to me? You are a black lady and I am white guy! I said to him, in the Kingdom of God there is not white or black. English or Uganda- African, God in heaven is our creator, we were all made in His Image: *Genesis 1: 26, then God said, " let us make mankind in our image, in our likeness, so that they may rule over fish in the sea and birds in the sky, rule over the livestock and all wild animals, and over all the creatures that move along the ground. We are God's creation. One God- one love.* in Him blood has no colours, it is just blood. There is no such thing as racism. (God is every one's race, if you go to Africa, God is there as, if you come to Britain, God is here as, go to North America, God is there as! You can't look for God as if you will find Him wrapped in two **colours** because you will never find Him. But if you are looking for Him or looking at Him as *love* then you will be able to find Him. So put that racism down and display love, because *love is* only one that matters and it is only one that is needed. If you feel like running a race, run the race of love but not a race of racism! I do not need to run around all day trying to convince another person that I, matter as if I do not know who and whose I am. And if you are calling it **black** there is nothing wrong with a person being **black but that is there a black person on earth as you think**! Black is beautiful, black is wonderful, black is awesome because God is Beautiful! And who carried the cross of Jesus? Simon of Cyrene! An African man. Do you want to say that him carrying Jesus' cross had something to do with his blackness?! I wish I was there at that time to carry it! You black, blessed and highly favoured! ***Matthew 27:32, And as they came out, they found a man of Cyrene, Simon by name, him they compelled to bear Jesus' cross.*** Goggle is telling me this man's origin is North-Africa! Because really, what is black? And what is white? Have you ever seen a white person before? I have vinegar never seen a white human being on earth! *I mean white as we call it! I have a white dress I know white!* I have a black dress and I have never a person as black as my black dress, may be...! Have ever seen white blood or black blood? I, mean blood in colour as it is? If an experiment was to be done, that one should put blood in a bottle, I mean from what you call *white person and what you call black person,* can you pick what is yours? Be reminded that the only thing that is missing is God's mind but we are made in God's image, not in God's images. So let us have God's mind towards one another. *Mark 12:31, Jesus teaching His disciples said, and you shall love your neighbour as yourself, there is no other commandment greater than this.* Racism is hatred, hatred is evil, love is good and beautiful because God is *good.* Don't be like that Pharaoh who decided to oppress the children of Israel because they were excelling, increasing

Exodus 1:7, but the children of Israel were fruitful and increased abundantly, multiplied and grew exceedingly mighty and the land was filled with them.

Exodus 1:9, and Pharaoh said, look the people of the children of Israel are more and mightier than us

Exodus 1:10, Come, let us deal wisely with them lest they multiply!

Exodus 1:12, So they set taskmasters over them, ***put, a knee on their neck, squeezed their neck with a knee*** *to afflict them with anger (burden) but the more they afflicted them, the more they multiplied and grew.*

Exodus 1:13, so the Egyptian made the children of Israel serve with rigour

. We are no longer in the days of Pharaoh but the same spirit that is still operating must die in Jesus' name. We need to be extra careful because God hears cry when you decide to oppress your brother or your sister with any type knee and make him or her cry, it makes God unhappy! Because,

In Exodus 3:6-8, I'm the God of your father- the God of Abraham, the God of Isaac and the God of Jacob and Moses hid his face for he was afraid to look upon God. God said I have surely seen the oppression of my people who are in Egypt and I have heard their cry because their taskmasters for I know their sorrows. So I have come down to deliver them from the hands of the Egyptians.

However I told him (my friend) that if you want me to go out with you, then I will take you to church (house of God.) He asked me again, do you dance in your church? And can I bring my beer, I told him, yes we dance for Jesus and we have a drink, refreshments (tea and coffee) He said, I want you to my girlfriend! I didn't think I heard him properly! I told his cousin to take care of him. His cousin said, I have talked to him many times but he refused to listen. Then one day I, happened to meet that man's family, they told me that he had given up on drink and he was in rehabilitation. I asked if I could visit but they asked me, who are you? Only family members were allowed. God heard my prayers! As my eleven years old son says, we need to tell people about Jesus and continue praying for them. As I also know that someone out there was praying for me. When I had just come to UK my baby cousin wrote a letter to me, it was a letter that I will never forget! He said, ***Dear Betty Amiina, I want to ask you, do you still love God? My advice to you is, if you leave God alone, He will also leave you alone!*** I can say that he was really ministered because who could have told him! God can use anyone to draw you to Himself. Don't keep Jesus to yourself, share Jesus, share love. I was once in bondage, in the middle of nowhere, but now I'm free. Since I received Jesus and received freedom. I must share Him with those who are yet to receive Him. I/ we have to make Jesus known to those who *don't* Him. Before I came to UK I used to hear one Ugandan gospel artist singing this song: ***Jesus set me free, I'm now ever free, Jesus set me free, I'm no longer a slave.*** *John 8:34-36, And them, "Most assuredly I say to you, whoever commits a sin is a slave to sin. And a slave does not abide in the house forever, but a son abides forever. Therefore if the Son sets you free, you are free indeed.* **2 Corinthians 5:17, Therefore if anyone is in Christ, he is a new creation, old things have passed a way, behold all things have become new.** So do not let anyone condemn you because some people love to condemn as if! Because *Romans 8:1-2, Therefore now no condemnation to those who are Christ Jesus, who do not walk according to the flesh, but according to the Spirit. For the law of the Spirit of life in Jesus has made me free from the law of sin and death.* Any way preach *Jesus*, preach Christ. Jesus is not someone you know and then keep to your self, you must share Jesus with others. It has to be a chain, others will also tell others. Think about it, Jesus came all way from heaven but we, we are here, so really we are not far from each other. We must empty hell and fill up heaven, wether we feel like or not, heaven has to be populated, Jesus' banquet Hall has to be filled up. Sometimes even without saying a word, one can evangelize, all you have to do is have light and remember you can't have light if you don't have love. Love is the main ingredient. The one who came from heaven is Love so He came to be the light of the world. I still remember that He said that things which He did we, shall do greater:

John 14:12, most assuredly I say you, he who believes in me the works that I do, he will do also, and greater works than these he will do because I'm going to Father.

OK, we cannot really have greater love than God but He left us a commandment, is love one another as I have loved you.

John 13:34-35, A new commandment I give to you, that you love one another as I have loved you. By this all will know that you my disciples if you have love for one another.

Even those who are hard to be loved! I'm glad that He did not say, be friend to everyone because some friends are *Judas* but we can still *love* them. Yes, they betrayed you and betrayed your trust but Jesus loved Judas till, Judas was the one who hanged himself because he could not take it. I'm surprised at Jesus' reaction the night that Judas gave Him a kiss!

Luke 22:48, But Jesus said to him, "Judas, are you betraying the Son of Man with a kiss?

Love is sweet, love is fire, and love is light, but when it's in you, do you have go around telling everyone, see, I have the light of God in me! Actions speak louder than words. If I really have the light of God in me I will not need to announce it to anyone, every one will see and know that I have the light of God in me. If I let it shine so bright people will want to come to it. First they will come to ask how I got it, they come because Jesus called us light! We are light in this world if we switch that light (love) on.

Matthew 5:14-16, He said, you are the light of the world, a *city that set on the hill cannot be hidden.*

15, nor do they light a lamp and put it under the basket but on a lampstand and it gives light to all who are in the house.

16, so, let your light so shine before men that they may see your good works and glorify your Father in heaven.

How can light be hidden? Unless you don't want it to shine! Love is a magnet that attracts, it causes attention. OK, I know that they are people out there who can't stand your light. Their stomach just grumbles whenever they see you doing good. But if you ever meet such, this is reason, it's because they can't stand that sweet spirit that in you and that why they react so bad each time they set their eyes on you. But I know that for sure, perfume can never attract flies. But just put garbage in the corridor and see flies dancing! So who has the power to change another? We all know that to eliminate the bad smell is to spray the opposite. Light has power to change darkness. In most cases when you are in the kitchen cooking, and that food brings out a beautiful aroma, don't you see people coming from every corner of the house to check out what you are cooking! It's because they have been attracted by that sweet aroma. OK, now burn that food by mistake, you will see that as soon as that bad smell get into their noses the first thing is to close their doors, while opening windows on the other side for fresh air to come in. To freshen up the whole house is too wash up, and spray air freshener not in the kitchen alone but, in the entire house. The Bible does say that kings shall came to your brightness.

Isaiah 60:3, Gentiles shall come you your light and Kings to the brightness of your rising.

One day back in 2012, I was out shopping then I decided to evangelize while doing shopping. Ok, I was new! I entered a shop and a man looked at me, "he asked," where is your baby? I answered, my baby is at home. And he concluded by saying," see, you have left your baby home to catch a man! And he asked me again," is this not the reason you changed your hair style? I answered, no, but I have come here to catch you for Jesus! He said, Jesus! I answered yes. After I, had done with shopping this man said, lovely, you are so happy! I said, thank you. Then he asked me, why are you so happy? I told him, I have Jesus. But I asked him, while showing him a leaflet in my hand, have I, ever given you one of these? He asked, what for? I answered, it's about Jesus. He said, " don't tell me about this Jesus, if it was God, I would have said yes. But Jesus, that man came to cause trouble, He is the reason why the world is full of trouble! I couldn't answer because I did not want to give a wrong answer. Then I said if Jesus is a troubled maker, He came to trouble satan but not you! I was told that Jesus, Him being a messenger makes Himself God! Still doing my evangelism I met this couple in town then I decided to tell to them about God. I gave a leaflet to the husband but the wife told me that they did not believe in God! I asked, why? Then, I said, Jesus loves you! This was back in 2012 may be I did not know how to approach people! The only word I knew is, Jesus loves you! But when I said Jesus loves you, this man removed his shirt and showed me a big tattoo on his chest and said, see, this is my God! When I saw it I said to him, "that is not God! When I said that he became very angry! Then his wife held his hand and said, let us go from here! They ran as if someone was running after them, but before that this man was screaming and that why is his wife had to say that. Whenever I, mentioned Jesus to him, the man would scream and say, take this from me, meaning the leaflet. A man screamed like a baby but I wondered why? It was somewhere in a corner shop. It was a scary moment but while talking to them I was not scared! Some people can be so aggressive after hearing this name, *Jesus!* This man became so angry and what made him angry is that I talked about the name *Jesus!* At some point he started shaking, I noticed it from the moment I gave him that leaflet but I thought may be his hands had problems! But the more I mentioned Jesus, the more he screamed, after some time he started shaking and said, take this from me, take this from me! I did not know why! The very moment that leaflet left his hand, he stopped shaking! What happened that day remained a mystery to me, how a man scream like a baby because I mentioned Jesus to him and gave him a church leaflet! But really, we can't stop talking about Jesus. Back then some people used to tell me that He is a trouble maker but because I, did not want to give them a wrong answer I would just keep quiet as if I did not hear what they said. I know Jesus is not a trouble maker. He is the Prince of peace but If He was to make any trouble what type of trouble would He create? Would He sit down and watch while satan is oppressing His children? Fire He is, in the kingdom of darkness, light in the darkness. The reason Jesus came forth was not to nurse satan, but it was to destroy the works of satan.

1 John 3:8, He who sins is of the devil, for the devil has sinned from the beginning, for this purpose the Son of God was manifested that He might destroy the works of satan.
I once received a song that says,

There destruction in the kingdom of darkness:

There is destruction in the kingdom of darkness.
There is destruction in the kingdom of darkness.
There is destruction in the kingdom of darkness.
Every work of satan shall be destroyed.
Every work of satan shall be destroyed.

The power of God is work, at Work.
The power of God is at work.
The power of God is at work.
Every work of satan shall be destroyed.
Every work of satan shall be destroyed,

The fire of God is at work, at work.
The fire of God is at work.
The fire of God is work.
Every work of satan shall be destroyed.
Every work of satan shall be destroyed.

Every tree my Father did not plant in me, shall be uprooted.
Every tree my Father did not plant in me, shall be uprooted.
Every work of satan shall be destroyed.
Every work of satan shall be destroyed.

There is destruction is the camp enemies.
There is destruction in the camp of enemies.
There is destruction is the camp of enemies.
Every work of satan shall be destroyed.
Every word of Satan shall be destroyed.

Every tree your Father did not plant in you, shall be uprooted.
Every tree your Father did not plant in you, shall be uprooted.
Every work of satan shall be destroyed.
Every work of Satan shall be destroyed.
End.

Jesus Himself does not cause any trouble, but the name Jesus does. It causes fire to the bad side and brings calmness to the other side, it brings freedom from oppression, demons free whenever His name is called. Jesus is the only name, it is above all names.

Philippians 2:9-11, therefore God has highly exalted Him and given Him a name which is above every name, that at the name of Jesus every knee should bow, of those in heaven and of those on earth, and of under and that every tongue should confess that Jesus Christ is Lord to the glory of God the Father. His name is life giver, story changer, His is a strong tower, His name so precious and so sweet. The name Jesus is fire, His name is beautiful, it is a sharp sword. What else can I say about the name Jesus. His name is forever Awesome, forever mighty! Forever glorious, forever wonderful. The name Jesus brings hope, in Jesus' name the lame walk, the blind receives sight, the mute speaks, the deaf hears. No barrenness in the name of Jesus. The name of Jesus is a rock, it is too Magnificent, forever Victorious, the name Jesus is available, free of charge it's purchased without money. Don't let any one sell prayers to you, don't buy!, there is a song that says, ***freely, freely, you have received, freely, freely give, go in my name because you believe, others will know that I live.***

Jesus said: *in Matthew 10:8, In my name heal the sick, cleanse the lepers, raise the dead, cast out demons, freely you have received freely give.* The only currency you needed is faith. Even if you call Jesus' name a thousand time and you have no faith it's all in in vain.

When Jesus was on Earth this is what He asked, ***do you believe I can do this? If a person said, yes, I believe, He would then say, let it be according your faith:*** *Matthew 8:13, then Jesus said to the centurion, "go your way and as you believed, so let be done for you and his servant was healed in that hour.*

A boy healed. *Mark 9:20–27, Then they brought him to Jesus and when he saw Him immediately the spirit conversed him and he fell to the ground and wallowed, forming at the mouth. So Jesus asked his father, "How long has this been happening to him?" And he said from childhood, and often it has thrown him both into the fire and into the water to destroy him but if you can if you can do anything, have compassion on us and help us. Jesus said to him, "if you can believe all things are possible to him who believes. the father of the child cried out and said with tears, "Lord, I believe, help my unbelief!" When Jesus saw that the people came running together, He rebuked the unclean spirit saying, "Deaf and dumb spirit, I command you, come out him and enter him no more. Then the spirit cried out convulsed him greatly and came out of him, and he became as one dead so that many said, "he is dead." But Jesus took* ***the boy*** *by the hand and lifted him up and he arose.*

Jesus said to her, your faith has made you well:

Luke 8:43:48, Now a woman having a flow of blood for 12 years, who had spent all liv hood on physicians and could not be healed by any. Came from behind and touched the boarder of His garment, and immediately her flow of blood stopped. Jesus said, who touched me?" When all denied it Peter and those with him said, "Master, the multitudes throng you and press you, and you say, "Who touched me?" But Jesus said, "somebody touched me, for I perceived power going out from me. Now when the woman saw that she was not hidden, she came trembling and falling down before Him in the presence of all the people the reason she had touched Him and how she was healed immediately. Jesus said to her, "daughter, be of good cheer, your faith has made you well, go in peace.

Jesus heals Blind Bartimaeus, (faith)

Mark 10:46-52, Then Jesus came to Jericho, and as He went out of Jericho with His disciples and a great multitude, blind Bartimaeus the son of Timaeus sat by the road side begging, and when he heard that it was Jesus of Nazareth, he began to cry out and say, Jesus, son of David, have mercy on me. Then many warned him to be quiet but he cried out the more, "Son of David have mercy on me!" So Jesus ***stood still*** *commanded him to be called, then the called the blind man saying to him, "Be of good cheer, rise, He is calling you. And throwing aside his garment, he arose and came to Jesus. And Jesus answered and said to him, what do you want me to do for you? The blind man said to Him, Rabboni, that I may receive my sights. Then Jesus said to him, go your way, you faith has made well, "And immediately, he received his sight and followed Jesus on the road.*

Jesus and the woman from Canaan:

Matthew 15:20-28, Then Jesus went out from there and departed to the region of Tyre and Simon. And behold, a *woman from Canaan came from that region and cried out to Jesus saying, have mercy on me O, Lord Son of David! My daughter is severely demon-* possessed. *But He answered her not a word, and His disciple came and urged Him saying, send her away for she cries after us. Jesus said, I was not sent except for the lost sheep of the house of Israel. Then she came and worshipped Him saying, Lord, help me! But Jesus answered and said, it's not good to take children's bread and throw it to the little dogs. And she said, "Truly Lord, yet even the little dogs eat the crumbs which fell from the Master's table. Then Jesus, answered and said to her, O, woman, great is your* ***faith!*** *Let it be as you desire, and her daughter was healed from that very hour.*

Jesus healed a paralytic carried by four men:

Mark 2:2-12, Immediately many gathered together so that there was no longer room to receive them. And they came to Him, bringing a paralytic who was carried by four men. And when they could not come to Him because of crowd, they uncovered the roof where He was. So when they had broken through, they let down the bed on which the paralytic was lying. When Jesus saw their faith, He said to the paralytic, "son, your sins are forgiven." But some of the scribes were sitting there and reasoning in their hearts, why does this Man speak blasphemies like this? Who can forgive sins but God alone?" And immediately when Jesus perceived their in His spirit that they reasoned, thus within themselves, He said to them, "Why do you reason about these things? Which easier, to say to the paralytic, "Your sins are forgiven, or to say, "Arise, take up your bed and walk? "But that you may know that the Sony of Man has power to forgive sins", He said to the paralytic, "I say to you, take up your bed and go to your house. And Immediately , he arose, took the bed and went out in the presence of them all, so that there were all amazed and glorified God, saying, we never seen anything like this !"

A man came to Jesus, kneeling down before Him and saying:

Matthew 17:14-21, And when they came to the Multitude, a man came to Jesus kneeling down to Him and saying, Lord, have mercy on my son, for He is an epileptic, and suffers severely for he often falls into the fire and often into the water. So I brought him to your disciples but they could not cure him. Then Jesus answered and said, "O faithless and perverse generation, how long shall I be with you? How long shall I bear with you? Bring him here to me,"

And Jesus rebuked the demon and it came out of him and the child was cured from that hour. Then the disciples came to Jesus privately and said, "why could we not cast the demon out? So Jesus said to them, because of your unbelief. However, this kind does not go out except by prayer and fasting.

I once heard song that says:

Everywhere He went He was doing good, Almighty hear, He healed lepers, when crippled saw Him, they started walking, every where He went My Lord was doing good!

Matthew 15:30-31, then great multitude came to Him, having with them those who were lame, blind, mute, maimed and many others and they laid them down at the Jesus' feet and He healed them.

31, so Multitude marvelled when they saw the mute speaking, the maimed made whole, the lame walking and the blind seeing. And the glorified the God of Israel.

Matthew 11 : 4-5, Jesus answered, go and tell John the things which you hear and see, 5, the blind receives their sight and the lame walk, the lepers are cleansed and the deaf hear, the dead are raised and poor have the gospel preached to them.

Many touched the hem of His garment and were made well.

Matthew 14:35-36, and when the men of that place recognised Him, they sent into all that surrounding region brought to Him all who were sick, and begged Him that they might touch the Hem of His garment. And as many as touched it were made perfectly well.

We are free, we are healed in Jesus' name, Amen, (so, let it be) Jesus the only name that is given to us:

A lame man healed:

Acts 3:1-10, Now Peter and John went up together to the temple tat the hour of prayer, the ninth hour.

2, And a certain man lame from his mother's womb was carried, whom they daily laid at the gate of temple which is called beautiful to ask alms from those entered the temple.

3, Who seeing Peter and John about to go to the temple asked alms.

4, And fixing his eyes on him, with John, Peter said, " look at us.

5, So he gave them attention expecting to receive something from them.

6, Then Peter said, "silver and gold I do not have, but what I have but what I have, I give you, in the name of ***Jesus Christ,*** *of Nazareth, rise up and walk.*

7, And he took him by the right hand and lifted him up and immediately his feet and ankle bones received strength.

8, So he, leaping up, stood and walked and entered the temple with walking and praising God.

Acts 3:9-10, And all the people saw him walking and praising God.

10, The they knew that it was he who sat begging alms at the beautiful gate of the temple, and they were filled with wonder and amazement at what had happened to him.

Peter and John arrested! For what?!

Acts 4:2-12, And being greatly disturbed that they taught the people and preached in Jesus' name and the resurrection from the dead.

3, They laid hands on one them and put them in custody until the next day, for it was already evening.

4, However, many of those who heard the word believed and the number of them came to be about five thousand.

5, And it came to pass, on the next day, that rulers, elders and scribers,

6, As well as Annas the high priest, Caiaphas, John and Alexander and as many as were of the family of the high priest gathered together at Jerusalem.

7, And when they had set them in them midst (Peter and John), they asked, "by what power or what name have done this?

10, Then Peter filled with the Holy spirit said to them, "Rulers of the people and elders of Israel.

9, If we this day judged for a good deed done to the helpless man by what means he has been made well.

10, let it be known to you all and to all the people of Israel, that by the name Jesus Christ of *Nazareth, whom you crucified, whom God raised from the dead by Him, this man stands here before you whole.*

11, This is the stone which was rejected by you builders, which has become the chief corner stone.

12, Peter said, nor is there salvation in other, for there is no other name under heaven given among men by which we must be saved.

The name Jesus is forbidden!

Acts 4:13-22 And when they saw the boldness of Peter and John, and perceived that they were uneducated and untrained men, they realized that they had been with Jesus!

14, And seeing a man who had been healed standing with them, they could say nothing against it.

16, but when they had commanded them to go aside, out of the council, they conferred among themselves, what shall we do to these men? That indeed a notable miracle had been done through them is evident to all who dwell in Jerusalem and we cannot deny it!

17, But so that it spreads no further among the people, let us severely threaten them that from now on they speak to no man in this name, (in Jesus' name)

18, And they called them and commanded them not to speak at all nor teach in the name of Jesus.

19, But Peter and John answered and said to them, Wether it is right in the sight of God to listen to you more than to God, you judge. For we can't but speak things which we have heard.

20, For we cannot but speak the things which we have seen and heard.

21, So when they further threatened them, they let them go, finding no way of punishing them because of the people, since they all glorified God for what had happened

22, For a man was over forty years old, on whom this miracle of healing had been performed.

A girl possessed with the spirit of divination delivered in Jesus' name:

Acts 16:16, It *happened* as *Paul and Silas were going for player that* a *certain slave girl possessed with* a *spirit of divination met them, who brought her masters much profit by fortune- telling.*

17, The girl followed Paul and Silas and cried out saying," these men are the servants of the Most High God, who proclaim to us the ways of salvation.

18, She did it for many days, but Paul greatly annoyed turned and said to the spirit, "I command you in the name of Jesus Christ to come out of her," and the evil spirit came out that very hour.

19, But when her masters saw that their hope of profit was gone, they seized Paul and Silas and dragged them into the marketplace to the authorities.

A crippled man healed in Jesus' name:

Acts 14:8-10, In *Lystra* a *certain man without strength in His feet was sitting,* a *cripple from his mother's womb, who had never walked. This man had Paul speaking, Paul observing him intently, and seeing that he had faith to be healed. Said with a loud voice, "stand up on your feet! And he leaped and walked.*

Miracles by the hand of Paul:

Acts19:11-12, God worked unusual miracles by hands of Paul, that even his handkerchiefs and aprons were brought from his body to the sick and the diseases left them and the evil spirits went out from them.

Warning! evil spirits and demons know who to obey, they know who is who! If you do not have Jesus in you, do not risk your life to cast out evil spirits.

Acts 19:13-16, Others took it upon themselves to call the name of the Lord Jesus over those who had evil spirits, saying, "we adjure you by this Jesus whom Paul preaches. Also there were seven sons of Sceva, a Jewish priest, who did so.

And the evil spirit answered and said, "Jesus, I know, and Paul, I know, but who are you?" The man in whom the evil spirit was, leaped on them and overpowered them and prevailed against them, so that they fled out of that house naked and wounded. This became known both to all Jews and Greeks dwelling in Ephesus and fear fell on them and the name of the Lord Jesus was magnified. And many who had believed cane confessing and telling their deeds, also many of them who had practiced magic brought their books together and burned them in the sight of all and they counted up the value of them and it totalled fifty thousand pieces of sliver. So the word of word of the Lord Jesus grew mightily and prevails.

When we read Bible we see that demons knew Jesus, in most cases they cried out and worshipped Him. **A demon - possessed man lived in tombs meets with Jesus:**

Mark 5:1-20, Then they came to other side of the sea, to the country of the Gadarenes , and when Jesus had come out of the boat, immediately there met Him out of the tombs a man with unclean spirit.

V3, he had his dwelling among the tombs and no one could bind him, not even with chains.

V4, he had often been bound with shackles and chains, and chains had been pulled apart by him and shackles broken in pieces, neither could any one tame him.

V5, Always night and day he was in the mountains and in the tombs crying out and cutting himself with stones.

*V6, **But** when he saw **Jesus** from far he ran and worshipped Him.*

*V7, and cried out with a loud voice and said, what have I, to do with you **Jesus,** Son of the Most High God? I, implore you by God that you do not torment me.*

*V8, For **Jesus** said to him," come out of the man, unclean spirit.*

V9, Then Jesus asked, "what is your name?" And he answered saying, my name is legion: for we are many.

V10, And he begged Jesus earnestly that He would not send them out of the country.

*Then v12, and all the demons begged **Jesus**, saying, send us to the swine, that we may enter them.*

V13, And at once Jesus gave them permission, then the unclean spirits went out and entered the swine, (there were about two thousand): and the hard ran violently down the steep place into the sea and drowned in the sea.

V14, Now those who fed the swine fled and told it in the city and in County...

*V15, Then they came to **Jesus** and saw the one who had been demon- possessed and had the legion sitting and clothed and in right mind, and they were afraid.*

V16, Those who saw it told them how it happened to him who had been demon-possessed and about the swine.

V17, Then they began to please to Jesus to depart from their region.

*Then v18, And when Jesus got into the boat, he who had been demon- possessed begged **Jesus** that he might be with **Him**.*

*V19, However, Jesus did not permit him but said to him, go **home** to **your friends** and **tell** them what **great things** the Lord has **done** for you and how He had compassion on you.*

*V20, And he departed and began to **proclaim** in **Decapolis** all that Jesus had done for him, and all marvelled.*

Mark 3:9-12**, Jesus healed many:**

V9, And Jesus told His disciples that a small boat should be kept ready for Him because of the Multitude, lest they should crush Him.

V10, For Jesus healed many, so that as many as had afflictions pressed about Him to touch Him.

V11, And the unclean spirits, whenever they saw Him fell down before Him and cried out, saying, "you are the Son of God.

V12, But Jesus sternly warned them that they should not make Him known.

Mark 1:21-28, **Jesus casts out an unclean spirit**

V21,Then they went into Capernaum and immediately on the sunbath Jesus entered the Synagogue and taught.

V22,And they were astonished at His teaching for He taught them as one having authority and not as the scribes.

V23, Now there was a man in their synagogue with unclean spirit and he cried out.

V24, Saying, "Let us alone! What have we to with you, Jesus of Nazareth? "Did you come to destroy us? I know who you are- the Holy one of God.

V25, But Jesus rebuked him, saying, "Be quiet and come out of him!

V26, And when the unclean spirit had convulsed him and cried out with a loud voice, he came out of him.

V27, Then they were amazed so that they questioned among themselves saying, "What is this is? For with authority He commands even the unclean spirit and they obey Him?

V28, And immediately His fame spread throughout all the region around Galilee.

Mark 1:32-34, many healed after the Sabbath:

V32, At the evening when the sun had set they brought to ***Jesus*** *all who were and those who were demon- possessed.*

V33, And the whole city was gathered at the door.

V34, And Jesus healed many who were sick with various disease and cast out many demons, and He did not allow demons to speak because they knew Him.

Mark 1:38-39, preaching in Galilee:

V38, *But Jesus said to them, "let us to go to the next towns that I may preach there also because for this purpose I have come forth.*

V39, And He was preaching in their Synagogues throughout all Galilee and casting out demons.

Mark 1: 40-45, **Jesus cleanses a leper**:

V40, Then a leper came to Jesus, imploring Him, kneeling down to Him and saying to Him, if you are willing you can make me clean.

V41, And Jesus moved with compassion put out His and touched him and said to him, be cleansed.

V42, As soon as Jesus had spoken, immediately the leprosy left him.

V43, And Jesus strictly warned him and sent him away at once.

V44, But Jesus said to Him, "Say that you say nothing to anyone: but go your way, show yourself to the Priest and offer your cleaning those things which Moses commanded as a testimony to them.

V45, He went out and began to proclaim it freely and spread the matter so that Jesus could no longer openly enter the city but was outside in deserted places and they came to Jesus from every quarter.

Mark 7:32-37, **Jesus heals a deaf mute:**

V31, And again departing from the region of Tyre and Sidon, Jesus came through the midst of the region of Decapolis to sea of Galilee.

V32, They brought to Jesus one who was deaf and had impediment in his speech and begged Him to put His hand on him.

V33, And Jesus took him aside from the multitude and put His fingers in his ears and He spat and touched his tongue.

V34, Then looking up to heaven Jesus sighed and said, "Ephphatha, that is be opened."

V35, Immediately his ears were opened and the impediment of his tongue was loosed and he spoke plainly.

V36, Then Jesus commanded them that they should tell no one but the more He commanded them, the more widely they proclaimed.

V35, And they were astonished beyond measure saying, He has done all things well, He makes both the mute and the deaf to hear and the mute to speak.

Mark 16:6, **Mary Magdalene:**

When Jesus had risen He appeared to Mary Magdalene, out of whom He had cast seven demons.

Mark 1:29-31, **Jesus healed Peter's mother in law:**

V29, As soon as they had come out of the Synagogue, they entered the house of Simon and Andrew, with James and John.

V30, But Simon's wife's mother lay sick with a fever and they told Him about her at once.

V31, So Jesus came and took her by the hand and lifted her up, and immediately the fever left her and she served Him.

John 5:2–13, **Jesus healed a lame man at the pool:**

V1, After this there was a feast of the Jews and Jesus to went to Jerusalem. V2, Now there in Jerusalem by the sheep gate a pool which is called in Hebrew, Bethesda, having five porches.

V3, In these lay great Multitude of sick people, blind, lame, paralysed, waiting for the moving of water.

V4, For an angel went down at a certain time into the pool and stirred up the water, then whoever stepped in first after the stirring of water was made well of whatever disease he had.

V5, Now a certain man was there who had an infirmity ***thirty eight years.***

V6, When ***Jesus saw*** *him lying there and knew that he already had been in that condition a long time, He said to him, "Do you want to be made well?*

V7, The sick man answered Him, "Sir, I have no man to put me into the pool, when the water is stirred up but while I'm coming another steps down before me.

V8, ***Jesus*** *said to him,* ***"Rise, take*** *up your bed and walk.*

V9, And immediately the man was made well, took up his bed and walked and that day was the Sabbath.

V10, The Jews therefore said to him who was cured, "It is not lawful for to carry your bed.

V11, he answered them, "He who made me well said to me, take your bed and walk.

And in v12, Then they asked him, who is the man who said to you, take up your bed and walk?

V13, But the one who was healed did not know who it was for Jesus had withdrawn a multitude being in the place.

V14, Afterwards ***Jesus*** *found him in the temple and to him, (the one who was healed), see you have been made well, since no more lest a worse thing come upon you.*

V15, Then the man departed and told the Jews that it was ***Jesus*** *who had made him well.*

A woman bent for eighteen years, *Luke 13:10-13.*

V10, Now Jesus was teaching in one of the synagogue on the Sabbath.

V11, And behold, the was a woman who had a spirit of infirmity eighteen years and was bent over and could in on way raise herself up.

V12, But when Jesus saw her, He called her to Him and said to her, "Woman, you are loosed from your infirmity."

V13, And He laid His hands on her, and immediately she was made straight and glorified God.

Luke 14:18-19 **Jesus said**:

V18, the spirit of the Lord is upon on me, because He has anointed me to preach the gospel to the poor, He has sent to heal the broken hearted. To preach deliverance to the captives and recovery of the sight to the blind, to at liberty those who are oppressed.

V19, to preach the acceptable years of the Lord.

Acts 10:38, *we also read, how God anointed Jesus of Nazareth with holy spirit and power, who went out doing good and healing all were oppressed by the devil, for God was with Him.*

Acts 5:12, Peter's shadow; through the hands of the apostles many signs and wonders were done among the people.

Acts 5:12-16, And through the hands of the apostles many sins and wonders were done among the people and they were all with one accord in Solomon's porch. Ye none of the rest dared you join them but the people esteemed them highly. And believers were increasingly added to the Lord, multitude of both men and women. They brought the sick out into the street and laid them on beds and couches that at least the shadow of Peter passing by might fall on some of them. And a multitude gathered from the surrounding cities of Jerusalem, bringing sick people and those who we tormented by unclean spirits and they were all healed.

My son composed this song!

We are going to rock this place for Jesus:
We gonna rock this place for Jesus.
We gonna rock this place for Jesus.
We gonna rock this place for Jesus.
We gonna rock this place for Him.

It was Jesus Himself who gave disciples power over unclean spirit. But we are the disciples of this generation and the same power is still at work because Jesus is the same.

Hebrews 13:8, Jesus Christ the same, yesterday, today and for every.

Revelations 1:8, He says, I am the Alpha and the Omega, the Begging, and the End, "Says the Lord, " Who is, Who was and Who is to Come, the Almighty.

Malachi 3:8, For I am the God Almighty, I do not change, therefore you sons of Jacob are not consumed.

As He was so He is and the same power is available in us the reason Jesus came was to destroy the works of satan, no wonder they called Him a trouble maker.

Galatians 6:17, from now on let no one trouble me, for I bare in my body the marks of the Lord Jesus.

I once received this song, because I carry you Jesus;

Thank you Jesus, thank you,
For being a Mighty warrior.
For being a Mighty warrior

Because I carry you Jesus, because I carry you Jesus.
Enemies bow before you.
Because I carry you, because I carry Jesus,
demons tremble before you.
Because I carry you Fire, because I carry you Fire,
demons free before you.

We have to know what was given to us, otherwise! In 2017,as I was preparing to fly to Uganda to see my father after living in England for sixteen years, people tried to stop me. One would call me from Uganda and say, Betty, if you know how witches are ready for you in the village! Another would text, don't take your child to the village, I saw it in a vision that something bad will happen to you and your child if you both go to the village! But I was here laughing! OK, I know that they are there but do I or did I have to fear witches and their crafts? I was already at Kigali airport forty-five minutes to Uganda waiting for my connection and someone started, are you still going to the village? There are ready for you! But I, over looked and Ignored! I said, first of all my father lives in the village and he is the reason I prepared this trip but people are trying to scare me! I said it's because they don't me! I'm not that same person who left Uganda sixteen years go! If witches are in the village waiting for me, I'm also ready for them! And I made sure that no one talked about that matter to me any again. One person said, I have to escort you to the village, but I was busy laughing, are you my angel?

Within me I was saying, you don't know me! But I went and came back because Greater is that is He that is in me, Greater is He that is in my son than those in my village.

Greater is He that is in me than who is in *the world, 1 John 4:4.*

Sending out the twelve disciples:

Matthew 10:1, And when He had called His twelve disciples to Himself, He gave the power over unclean spirits, to cast them out and to heal all kinds of sickness and diseases.

Matthew 10:7–9, Jesus told them, as you go, preach saying, the Kingdom of God is at hand, heal the sick, cleanse the lepers raise the dead, cast out demons. Freely you have received, freely give.

Luke 10:19-20, Jesus, said, behold, I give you the authority to trample on serpents and scorpions and all the powers of the enemy and nothing shall by no means hurt you. Nevertheless, do not rejoice in this that the spirits are subjected to you but rejoice rather that your names are written in heaven.

Because the seventy were rejoicing: *Luke 10:17, Then the seventy returned with joy saying, Lord, even demons are subjected to us in* ***your*** *name.*

Psalm 91:13, I, shall tread upon the lion and the cobra, the young lion and the serpents, I shall trample under foot. It's time we understanding of this verse, as read it everyday I picture myself stepping on those cobras/ walking over them.

Mark 16:17–18, and Jesus said to them, "go into the whole world and preach the gospel to every creature.

16, He who believes and is baptised will saved, but he who does not believe will be condemned.

17, And these signs shall follow those who believe, in my name they shall cast out demons, they shall speak with new tongues.

18, they will take up serpents and if they drink any deadly, it will by no means hurt them, they will lay hands on the sick and they will recover.

Acts 9:36, Peter raises Dorcas from dead, in Joppa there was a certain disciple, Tabitha by name, which means Dorcas, this woman was full good works and charitable deed which she did.

Acts 9:37, but it happened that she became sick and died, when they had washed her, they laid her in the upper room.

Verse 39, then Peter and went with them, (two men who were sent in verse 38) when he had come they brought him to the upper room, and all the widows stood by him weeping, showing him the tunics and garments which Doncaster had made while she was with them.

V40, but Peter put them all out and knelt down and prayed, and turning to the body he said, Tabitha, arise! And she opened her eyes and when she saw Peter, she sat up.

Aeneas healed, *acts 9:32*

Aeneas healed, *acts 9:32-35,*

32, now it came to pass as Peter went through all parts of the country that he also came down to the saints who dwelt in Lydda.

33, there he found a certain man named Aeneas who had been bedridden eight years and was paralysed.

34, and Peter said to him, "Aeneas, Jesus heals Christ you. "Arise and make your bed, then he arose immediately.

35, so all who dwelt in Lydda and Sharon saw him and turned to the Lord.

There is no other name, only the name of Jesus

just call upon the name, I was inspired to write such songs;

The name of Jesus' is so mighty, the name of Jesus, is so powerful.
The name of Jesus, is so mighty, the name of Jesus, is so powerful
The name of Jesus has power, to set you free from the bondage.
The name of Jesus has power to save.
just call upon the name of Jesus.
Just call upon the name, just call upon the name.
Just called upon the name of Jesus.

The greatest weapon over Satan, is the of Jesus.
The greatest weapon over satan is the name of Jesus.

Hit, hit satan with the name of Jesus.
Hit, hit satan with the name of Jesus.
Crash, crash satan with the name of Jesus
Crash, that satan with the name of Jesus.

Hit that enemy with the name of Jesus.
Bang that enemy with the name of Jesus
Hit, hit sickness, with the name of Jesus.

Hit, hit barrenness with the name of Jesus.
Hit, hit laziness with name of Jesus.
End.

The Man of war is Jesus;

The Man of is Jesus,
The Man of war is Jesus,
The Man of war is Jesus.
Is Jesus, is Jesus, Mighty in battle.
Is Jesus, is Jesus, Jehovah Nissi.
Is here, is here, to destroy the work of satan.
Is here, Jesus is here, to destroy the works of satan.
Is here, Jesus is here, to disorganise the plans for satan.
The Man of war is Jesus.
The Man of war is Jesus.
End.

There is a name I love:

There is a name, I love, and it's so wonderful to me.
There is a name I praise and it's so wonderful to me.
There is a name I trust and it's so wonderful to me.

That name is so precious,
That name is so beautiful
that name powerful and mighty.
Do you know the name I'm talking about.
I am talking about the name of Jesus.

In that name, strength we receive.
In that name, the lame walk.
That name so real, that name is so real.
That name for me.

Jesus, Jesus, your name is enough for me.
Jesus, Jesus, your name is enough for me.

There is no other name, that I can call,
In time trouble and work for me.
There is no other name, that I can call,
In times of trouble and work for me.
Only the name, oh, the name of Jesus.
Jesus, Jesus, your name is enough for me.
Jesus, Jesus, the name is enough for me.
Your name is my hiding place,
Your name is my Tower.
Jesus, Jesus, the name of Jesus.

It's so, so sweet, sweet to my tongue,
It is a sword, to cut my enemy.
The name of Jesus,
I boast in the name of Jesus.

I have a name, that I boast in,
When the enemy is rising,
And he thinks he can win me.
All I have to do, is call that name of Jesus.
And the enemy will run away.

Jesus, Jesus, your name is enough for me.
Jesus, Jesus, your name is enough for me.

I have hope for tomorrow, because of the name of Jesus.
Tomorrow will be alright, because of the name of Jesus.

Jesus, Jesus, your name is enough for me.
Jesus, Jesus, your name is enough for me.

I will praise that name,
I will bless that name.
I will worship that name.

Jesus, Jesus, your name is enough for me.
Jesus, Jesus, your name is enough for me.

Other trust in their chariots,
They think they have horses.
I know where my trust is,
My trust is in the office Jesus.
Tomorrow will be alright, because I know the name of Jesus.
His name is so powerful, I'm talking about the name of Jesus.
Oh the name of Jesus, is enough for me.
Jesus your name, your name, is enough for me.
Jesus your name, your name is enough for me.
End.

I'm borrowing my son's song, thank you Isaiah for writing this song!

I **love that name**:

I love that name, I love that name,
I love that name, so much!
I love that name, I love that name,
I love that name, so much!

The name of Jesus, the name of Jesus,
I love that name, so much!

There is power in the name, there is power in the name.
There is power in the name of Jesus.
I love that name, I love that name.
I love that name, so much!
End.

For a reason, I sang this song, there is a story behind every song!

I'm a winner in the name of Jesus;

In the name of Jesus, I'm a winner, (chorus)
I'm a winner in the name of Jesus.
In the name of Jesus I'm a winner,

I'm a winner in the name of Jesus.
Let God arise, on my behalf,
Let God arise, on my behalf.
Let King arise, on my behalf.
I'm a winner in the name of Jesus.
Chorus)

There is no other name I can hope in.
There is no other name I can believe in.
There is no other name I can trust in.
Only the name of Jesus.
There is no other name I can fight with.
There is no other name I can use.
On the name of Jesus.
Chorus)

The name of Jesus is my sword.
The name of Jesus is my hiding place.
The name of Jesus is my shield.
Only the name of Jesus.
Chorus)

If I have lost before,
It's because I did not the name of Jesus,
Now I know the name, I will never lose a battle.
I will win, I will win, in the name of Jesus.
Chorus) end.

Victory all the way, the battle is won;

Victory all the way, Victory, victory all the way,
I sing, victory, victory all the way.
I shout victory, Victory all the way.
Oh, The battle is won in the name of Jesus.
Oh, The battle is won in the name of Jesus.

I praise you God for victory.
I praise you God for victory.
I praise you God for victory.
Oh, the battle is won in the name of Jesus.
Oh, the battle is won in the name of Jesus.

I thank you God for victory.
I thank you God for victory.
I thank you God for victory.
Oh, the battle is won in the name of Jesus.
Oh, the battle is won in the name of Jesus.

I bless you God for victory.
I bless you God for victory.
I bless you God for victory.
Oh, the battle is won in the name of Jesus.
Oh, the battle is won in the name of Jesus.
End.

Jehovah you are my portion, I will never be defeated;

- Jehovah you are my portion, you are my portion every day.
I will never be defeated, you are my portion.
I will never be defeated, you are portion.

You make me a conquer, Jesus.
I'm a winner every day, I will never be defeated.
You are my portion.
In you I live and have my being,
King of glory, I will never be defeated.
You are my portion.

Hallelujah, Jehovah you are my portion,
You are my portion every day, I will never be defeated.
You are my portion.
End.

I wrote this song in a conversation with God, you will show your power Jesus!

You will show your power, Jesus,
You will show your power, Jesus.
You will show your power, Jesus.

I look in front of me, I look in front of me,
I look around, I don't see anyone.
Who can help me, except you, Jesus,
You will show your power.
End

One day I was in my kitchen cooking and a song came to my spirit, thought God knows how I have cried!

you not cry again;

Let met tell you, you are crying to much!
I know that you are crying too much!
I know that you are crying too much!
every morning when you wake up your pillow is all soaked with water!
like you had a shower!
Like you had a shower!
But let me remind you, in all you are going through, you are not alone,
someone so big is with you, is watching over you,
so don't cry, don't cry, wipe tears from your eyes.
So don't cry, don't cry, wipe tears from your eyes.

So don't cry, don't cry, Jesus said it's enough!
So don't cry, don't cry, Jesus said, enough!

You will not cry again, Jesus said it's enough (chorus) ×2
You will not cry again, Jesus said it's enough!
He heard your cry, He heard your cry,
Jesus, said it's enough!
He heard your cry, He heard your cry,
Jesus, said, it's enough!

It's not over until He says it's over!
It's not until He says, it's over!
Satan has no power on you,
He can try but he cannot win.
Someone so- Big is with you.
His name is Jesus, His name is Jesus.
The only one that has power over you.
satan is a liar, a loser and a deceiver!
He has no power on you!

(×2 Chorus) you will not cry again, Jesus said, it's enough!
You will not cry again, Jesus said, it's enough!
You will not cry again, Jesus said, it's enough!
He heard your cry, He heard your cry.
Jesus said, enough!
He heard your cry, He heard your cry.
Jesus said, it's enough!
That sickness, you have, Jesus said you are healed.
His blood is cleansing you right now.
Just believe, drink the blood of Jesus.
Just believe, drink the blood of Jesus.

(×2 Chorus) you will not again, Jesus said it's enough!
You will not cry again, Jesus said enough!
He heard your cry, He heard your cry.
Jesus said, it's enough!
He heard your cry, He heard your cry,
Jesus said, enough.

In every trial, in every temptation.
May be you are left alone.
And you think nobody cares!
Let me assure you, Jesus cares about you.

(×2 Chorus) you will not cry again, Jesus said it's enough!
You will not cry again, Jesus said it's enough!
He heard your cry, He heard your cry,
Jesus said, it's enough!
He heard your cry, He heard your cry,
Jesus said, it's enough!
End.

I received this song in 2015, at first, the song did not make sense! Any way, sometimes things of God do not make sense to man! But then He is God, He knows The song came through my mouth but these words were not mine! They came from God-Love, the expert in mending a broken heart. But who broke my heart in the first place? I pray that it shall forever be well with him! May he never experience or see brokenness! May it forever be well with him and his family, in Jesus' name.

This song came as a medicine songs are medicines, it depends on how you apply it or use it!

Yet I received another song, but who was speaking? God or me? I gladly received it, I remember that I was in my kitchen cooking, my favourite place in the entire house, in fact I call my kitchen, office! I recorded the song on my phone, after listening to it, I thought it could be a healing song! But was I sick at that time?! I remember receiving these words.

Carpenter Jesus;

Carpenters Jesus, repair my life.
Carpenter Jesus, build my life
Jesus, I'm broken, I'm bleeding inside.
Jesus, heal these wounds and make me whole again!
End.

I said carpenter Jesus! What kind of word is this? Then I said, it's God, He sees where we cannot see, I said, could it be that I have wounds somewhere! It could be that I'm bleeding but I do not it! If not physical wounds then spiritual wounds! *But I should have known that I was broken! May be I did not want you admit it!*

I spent time meditating on the same, at the end I called this lady (Pastor) I told her, then she said that it does not mean that every song I receive is mine or has something to do with me! She said it could be a word for someone out there, so don't think that every song you receive from God has something to with only you!

He will answer you, very soon!

Good morning, I greet you all.
Good morning, I greet you all.
I have woken up today with a word of encouragement.
I have woken up today, with a word of encouragement.
Because I know, you are about to give up!
Because I know, you are thinking of giving up.
Don't give up, Jesus is here, oh,
Don't give up, Jesus is here, oh,
He will answer you, very, very soon, I know,

He will answer you, oh, very, very soon.
He will answer you, oh, very, very soon.
He will answer you, very, very soon.

He is making a way for you, where there no way.
He is cutting a way for you, where there is no way for you.
He is making a new thing, He is creating a new thing for you.

He will answer you, oh, very, very soon.
He will answer you, oh, very, very soon.
He will answer you, very, very soon.

I almost gave up but I held on to Him!
I almost gave up but I held on to Him!

He will answer you, very, very soon.
He will answer you, very, very soon
He will answer you, very, very soon.
End.

As I sat on a bus taking my son to school this song came to me, so recorded it on my phone while on a bus! ***You will make it!***

-You will make it, oh yes, you can do it.
Do not give up, do not lose hope.
Jesus is here to help you.
You will make it, do not give up.

That mountain, seems so from you.
All the dreams, you have been dreaming.
Do not give up, do not lose hope.
You will make it oh, yes, you can do it.

Don't you know, you are almost there?
Don't you know, you are almost there,
Don't you know? Do not lose hope!
Jesus is here, to help you cross to the other side.
He will help you cross to the other side.
End.

You can call a brother, or may be a friend but who can be like Jesus ? This is was word was for me, I did not doubt. Where does my help come from? *Psalm 121:1-2.*

I, don't know nobody;

You can talk from morning till tomorrow.
You can talk from morning till, tomorrow.
Oh, you can tell a brother, you can call a friend.
If you have a problem, or something is worrying you.
You feel like you want to talk to someone.
You make a phone call, you make a phone call.
You tell them how you feel, may be someone will help you!

But Let me tell you, I don't know nobody,
I don't know nobody, I don't know nobody,
No one, no one, who can help you like Jesus!

Chorus) I don't know nobody, who will be there for you!
I don't know nobody, who will be there for you!
No one, no one, who can help you like Jesus.

In every trial, in every temptation,
May be you are left alone,
May be you think, no one cares!
Let me assure you, Jesus cares about you.

Is it a brother or a sister.
You are telling about everything.
Nobody care for you, nobody cares for you.
Nobody cares for you!

That is the real truth, I'm telling you.
Every one is minding his own business.
They all mind their own businesses.
I don't anybody except, He is the one cares about you.
Chorus)

If Jesus never cares about you,
If He never cares about you,
Why did He came into this world?
Can your brother die for you?
Can your friend die for you?
Or can your sister die for you?
I don't know nobody, except Jesus.
I don't know nobody, who can help you like Jesus.
Chorus)
End.

The garment of Jesus is around, **touch the garment of Jesus**, ***receive your healing***;

Everybody, everybody, wherever you are,
Everybody, everybody, whatever you are doing,
Stretch out your hands in faith,

Stretch out your hands in faith,
Touch the garment of Jesus.

The garment of Jesus is around,
The garment of Jesus is around.
Touch the garment of Jesus.
Touch the garment of Jesus.
Receive your healing today.

There is power, there is power in the garment of Jesus.
There is anointing, there anointing in the garment of Jesus.
There is healing, there is healing in the garment of Jesus.
Oh touch the garment of Jesus.

It doesn't matter, how long you have been bleeding,
It doesn't matter, how long you have been bleeding.
Touch the garment of Jesus.
Touch the garment of Jesus.
Receive your healing today.
Receive your healing today.
End.

Those who trust in Jesus, nothing shall be impossible for them to do.

Tomorrow will be alright;

Tomorrow will be alright, tomorrow will be alright.
Our Redeemer lives.
His hands are not short that He cannot save.
His eyes are not blind that He cannot see.
His ears are not deaf that He cannot hear.
Nothing is impossible for Him to do.

All things are possible.
All things are possible.
All things are possible with Jesus.

And those who trust in Him, nothing shall be impossible for them to do.
Those who trust in Jesus, nothing shall be impossible for them to do.
Those who trust in Jesus, nothing shall be impossible for them to do.

All things are possible.
All things are possible.
All things are possible with Jesus.
End.

No matter what you are going through, don't lose hope, *He will make a way for you*:

He will make way, He will make a way, (chorus)
He will make a way for you.
He will make a way, He will make a way,
He will make a way for you.

No matter what you are going through.
Do not lose hope, God is on the Throne.
No matter what are going through.
Do not lose hope, God is on the Throne.
You will make it, He will help you, is in control
You will make it, He will help you, is in control
Chorus) He will make a way, He will make a way,
He will make a way for you.
He will make a way, He will make a way,
He will make a way for you.

If you have never seen rivers in desert, let me tell you it will start with you!
Because every desert in your life God will rivers of water,
Because every desert in your life God will make it rivers of water.
"let me tell you,
Chorus) He will make a way, He will make a way,
He will make a way for you.
He will make a way, He will make a way,
He will make a way for you.

Stand still and see the salvation of the Lord!
Stand still, do not shake and see the salvation of the Lord.
Chorus) He was make a way, He will make a way,
He will make a way for you.
He will make a way, He will make a way,
He will make a way for you.
End.

In most cases God shows up in the middle of our praises, sometimes the only way is through praise. Praise is a very powerful weapon, the moment I discovered a weapon of praise, I discovered my victory. When someone is just a complainer that what you do is complain, you fit perfectly at devil's seat! You become his friend because you are contributing to his ideas but the moment you switch from complaint to praises, you become too big for his sit, you can no longer fit. In as much as God loves our praises so devil hates praises because it creates trouble his camp, him and his agents cannot stand it. When we sing praises to God, the fire of God goes in for searching where those evil spirits and demons may be hiding. Praise is just fire in that kingdom. If someone is going through tough situation, be rest assured that God knows and He sees. OK, I know that it's hard to recognise God in the middle of storms and it can be hard to think that God is there and that why we can't hear Him even when He speaks to us! There was a time I felt this way everywhere I looked, if someone had told me that God was actually in heaven and that He loves, I would have called that person a big liar! When I finally came to my senses I knew that I had been thinking foolishly, God had never stopped caring. There was no point trying to ask myself if God had forgotten me, asking foolish and childish questions when I could have put on that weapon of praise. And said;

Father Lord God, I thank you, King of glory, I bless your holy name. Master planner Jesus, I magnify you, Ancient of days, Beautiful Saviour I adore you. How can I say thank you enough Jesus! Where can I start? Or where can I, end? I don't think I can mention all that you have done for me! My All in All Jesus take all the glory. What you have done, no one can do! Because you are God all by yourself. You are so powerful, you are the one with the ability final say. Who is he to open that door when you have already closed it? And who is he to shut when you open? Jesus, you are so good to me,

I just can't tell it all! You are so amazing, you are so Great and worthy of my praise. You do wonders, Awesome is your name, and Awesome are the works of your hand. You dried the red Sea for me. You gave me a song, I can now sing, no limitations in the name of Jesus. When foes said, I will never make it, when they all ganged up together and said, I will never cross to the other side, they did not know that my God is too Big and when it comes to fight, no one can stand Him! As I sometimes love talking to myself, one day I asked myself, can a dead person feel this way? I'm talking about some years back! I said, what if there was no breath in me, could I have felt this pain! I stood in front of a mirror and told God to forgive me, I said God forgive that person in the mirror.

No matter what comes to my way!

I will praise you, Jesus, I will praise you.
I will praise you, no matter what comes to my way.
I will praise you, no matter what comes to my way.
No matter what I see, Jesus, I will praise you
No matter what I hear, I will praise you.
No matter how I feel, Jesus, I will praise you.
I will praise you, no matter what comes to my way.
I will praise you, no matter what comes to my way.
End

In a song I once told God, if you never do anything else for me, Jesus, you have enough!

One more time Lord I, want to say thank you;

One time Lord, I want to say thank you! (chorus)
One more time Lord, I want to say thank you!
One more time Lord, I want to say thank you!
For all you have done, for all you have done, for all you have done.
One more time Lord, I want to say thank you!

And if you never, never do anything for me,
Jesus, you have done, you have enough, you have done enough!

If you never, never do anything for me,
Jesus, you have done enough! You have done enough!
You have done enough, I want to say thank you
You have done enough, I want to say thank you

For waking me up, every morning,
For journey mercies, I go out and come back in Jesus,
Your hand, your hand,
Your hand has protect me, Jesus, I want to say thank you!

Chorus) one more time Lord, I want to say thank you.
One more time Lord, I want to say thank you.
One more time Lord, I want to say thank you.
For all you have done, for all you have, for all you have done.
One more time Lord, I want to say, thank you!

You gave my life and new meaning, Jesus, you shook me from the dust.
You gave my life and new meaning, Jesus, you shook me from the dust.
Jesus, I was forgotten, you remembered me, Jesus,
You opened your book of rememberence, Jesus,
One time Lord, I want to say thank you!

I want to say thank you Jesus, for healing, for healing, for healing Jesus,
I want to say thank you, Jesus,
How can ever thank you enough, Jesus,
For carrying that cross for me, for carrying that cross for me!
You died with sinners, Jesus, because of me!
Oh, Jesus, you shed your blood to cleanse me.
Oh, Jesus, you shed your blood to heal me.
Oh, Jesus, you shed your blood to give me victory, hallelujah!
You shed your blood to give me victory, hallelujah, oh,
Jesus, I want to say thank you!
One time Lord, I want to say thank you!

I appreciate you, I appreciate you, I appreciate you with all my heart.
I appreciate you, I appreciate you, I appreciate you with all my heart.

One more time Lord I want to say thank you!
End.

I will sing His goodness, because His love has kept me, so when you see me shouting, you have to know that it is because of what He has done for me, I cannot help it but to praise this big God.

My heart is fully of Joy:

- My heart is full of joy, I'm dancing for Jesus.
He has done me well, I will praise Him forever more.
My heart is fully of joy, I'm singing for Jesus.
He has done me well, I will praise Him forever more.

When I think of my big God, and what He has done for me.
I cannot hid my praise, I cannot hide my praise.

When you see me dancing, when you see me singing,
When you see me jumping, when you see me shouting,
When you see me clapping, when you see me laughing,

You must know, you must know, it's because of what He has done for me!
I cannot help it, I cannot help myself, but to praise this big God.
But to praise this big God.

I'm so glad, I'm so glad, Jesus is my big God.
I'm so glad, I'm so glad, Jesus is my big God.
Because I had waited for a long time inside me I was doubting,
will He ever do it for me? Will He ever do it for me?
But when I came to my senses, I looked around, I looked around.
I didn't see any one, any one bigger than my God!

I was talking to myself, and I said but this big God,
He has never, never lied, He has never, never failed,
He has never lost any battle, how can He start with me?

I raised my hands and said Jesus, from now my hopes are in you.
Jesus, I'm in your hands, I'm tired of doing things the way I want them to be.

And nothing comes out.
I'm tired of fighting my battles and I have no power to fight!
The moment I put my trust in Him, that when He helped me.
Let me tell you, let me tell you,
Jesus knows our belief in Him.
Jesus knows our belief in Him.
End,

You gave my life a new meaning, *I will dance for you:*

You gave my life a new meaning, you gave my life a new meaning.
You gave my life a new meaning.
Oh Jesus, I will dance for you, I will dance for you,
I will lift you higher Jesus.

You turned my life around, you turned my life.
You turned my life around, Jesus.
Oh, Jesus I will dance for you, I will dance for you.
I will lift you higher Jesus.

You turned my mourning into dancing, you turned my mourning into dancing.
You turned my mourning into dancing,
Oh, Jesus I will dance for you, I will dance for you.
I will lift you higher Jesus.
End.

When I, look in front of me, I, see someone guiding my steps, *I know that is Jesus!*

- When I look, when I look, when I look in front of me, I see someone guiding my steps×2
Chorus) I know, I know, I know, yes, I know, I know that is Jesus.
I know, I know, I know, I know, yes, I know, I know that is Jesus.

He goes before me and make all crooked way straight.
He guide me, yes He guides me, as a Shepherd guiding his flocks.
Chorus) I know, I know, I know, yes, I know, I know that is Jesus.
I know, I know, I know, yes, I know, I know that is Jesus.

When I'm about to fall into the pit, He holds my hands and brings back.
When I'm about to fall into trouble, He comes by and brings back.
Chorus) I know, I know, I know, yes, I know, I know that is Jesus.
I know, I know, I know, yes, I know, I know that is Jesus.

When danger is a head of me, because He cares so much about me,
He warns me, my child, don't go that side.
When trouble is a head of me, because He loves so much,
He tells me, my child, don't go that way, and I know that is Jesus.
Chorus) I know, I know, I know, yes, I know, I know that is Jesus.
I know, I know, I know, yes, I know, I know that is Jesus.

He protects me day and night,
He Protects in and out,
He protects me to and from.
Chorus) I know, I know, I know, yes, I know, I know that is Jesus.
I know, I know, I know yes, I know, I know that is Jesus.
End.

When I face many challenges, and I. know where to turn to, I. know my Jesus will help me;

- *Thank you oh Lord, Thank you oh Lord, thank you oh Lord, you have done much, (chorus)*
In my life, in my life, in my life, you have done much!

You will never leave, oh Jesus, you will help me, oh, Jesus,
Every day, I call on you, you answer me you have done much!
You have done much Jesus, in my life
Chorus) thank you oh Lord, thank you oh Lord, you have done much.
In my life, in my life, in my life you have done much.

When I'm down Jesus, you tap me, you tap my shoulder and you tell me,
Don't worry, don't lose hope, I care about you,
You have done much Jesus, in my life.

You have done much Jesus, in my life.
Chorus) thank you oh Lord, thank you oh Lord, you have done much.
In my life, in my life, in my life, you have done much.

When I face many challenges, and I don't where to turn to,
I know my Jesus, will help me,
you have done much Jesus in my life.
You have much Jesus, in my life.
Chorus) thank you oh Lord, thank you oh Lord, you have done much.
In my life, in my life, in my life, you done much.

I thank you Jesus and I love you Jesus, because I know when I'm with you,
I'm safe in your hand. Who can touch your eyes Jesus?
Who can put a finger in your eyes? I'm the apple of your eye.
You have done much Jesus, in my life.
You have done much Jesus, in my life.
Chorus) thank you oh Lord, thank you oh Lord, you have done much.
In my life, in my life, in my life, you have done much.

Jesus, you have me in the palm of your hand,
When you see your hand, you see me.
It's an assurance that you love me,
And I know, no harm will ever befall me.
You have done much Jesus, in my life.
You have done much Jesus, in, my life.
Chorus) thank you oh Lord, thank you oh Lord, you have done much.
In my life, in my life, in my life, you have done much.

I wonder Jesus, I wonder Jesus.
I wonder Jesus, the love you have for me is unspeakable,
A love too much to talk about!
I cannot understand how you love me.
I thank you Jesus, and I praise you Jesus.
You have done much Jesus, in my life.

You have done much Jesus, in my life.
Chorus) thank you oh Lord, thank you oh Lord, you have much.
In my life, in my life, in my life, you have much.

When I go astray you always find me.
You bring me back in you house.
You tell me every day, don't worry my child,
I will help you, and I'm grateful Jesus.
You have done much Jesus, in my life.
You have done much Jesus, in my life.
Chorus) thank you oh Lord, thank you oh Lord, you have done much.
In my life, in my life, in my life, you have done much.

You will never leave nor forsake me,
That is your promise to me oh Jesus.
When I'm low, you stretch your hand towards and you lift me.
And I know Jesus, you care about me.
You have done much Jesus, in my life.
You have done much Jesus, in my life.
Chorus) thank you oh Lord, thank you oh Lord, you have done much.
In my life, in my life, in my life, you have dove much.
End.

You see me through every day, you help me every day;

- Take a look me, take a look at me.
And see what Jesus has done in my life!
Take a good look at me, take a good look at me!
See what Jesus has done in my life.

Thank you Jesus, thank you daddy.
Thank you Jesus, every day,
Thank you Jesus, every day.

You see through, every day, you help me every day,
Thank you Jesus, every day.
Thank you Jesus, every day.

You fight my battles and I hold my peace ×2
Thank you Jesus, every day.
Thank you Jesus, every day.

I will praise you, I will adore you.
I will worship you, I will honour you.
Thanks giving and adoration, be onto you forever more.
Thank you Jesus, every day.
Thank you Jesus, every day.

You shook me from dust, you sat me with Princes.
How can I ever thank you Father!
Thank you Jesus, every day.
Thank you Jesus, every day.

You are the only God I know, I will always glorify you.
There is no one in my heart, who can take your place.
Thank you Jesus, every day.
Thank you Jesus, every day.
End.

- What He does nobody can ask Him, Jesus, what are you doing?

Shout hallelujah, shout hallelujah
Shout Hallelujah, shout hallelujah, my Jesus reigns.
Hallelujah, my Jesus reigns.

King of glory reigns, King of glory reigns.
King of glory reign, shout hallelujah my Jesus reigns.
Hallelujah my Jesus reigns.
Hallelujah my Jesus reigns.

King of glory reigns, King of glory reigns,
Adonai reigns
Shout hallelujah my Jesus reigns.
Hallelujah my Jesus reigns.
Hallelujah my Jesus, reigns.

He is only one I know, who has the final say,
What He does nobody can ask Him, Jesus, what are you doing?
He is only one I know, who has the final say,
What He says nobody can ask Him, Jesus, what are you saying?
Hallelujah my Jesus reigns,
Hallelujah my Jesus reigns.

They call Him unquestionable, nobody can question Him!
They call Him unquestionable, you cannot disagree with Him!
They call Him unquestionable, nobody can question Him!
Hallelujah my Jesus reigns,
Hallelujah my Jesus reigns.

He has the power, oh, to do impossible.
He brought Lazarus back to life again.
Hallelujah my Jesus reigns.
Jesus told Martha, just believe,
And you will see the glory of God!
Hallelujah my Jesus reigns.
Hallelujah my Jesus reigns.

Jesus commanded, take away the stone!
They answered, Master, right there is a stench!
Jesus told them again, if you believe, you will the glory of God.
Hallelujah my Jesus reigns.
Hallelujah my Jesus reigns.

Jesus thanked His Father and called, Lazarus come out!
A man who was dead and buried four days came out at once!
Though he majestically walked out from the grave.
There was still a problem!
He was bound, he was bound with grave clothes.
He was bound, he was bound with grave clothes.
Jesus, commanded, loose him and let him go!

Jesus, commanded, loose him and let him go.
Hallelujah my Jesus reigns.
Hallelujah my Jesus reigns.

So whatever has tied you down, Jesus is commanding!
Loose him and let him go! Loose her and let her go!
Loose him and let marry! Loose her and let her marry!
Loose him and let him have children! Loose her and let her have children!
Loose him and let him make money! Loose and let make money!
You devil, loose him and let him go! Loose her and let her go!
Hallelujah my Jesus reigns.
Hallelujah my Jesus reigns.

You are no longer bound, Jesus has set you free!
You are no longer bound, Jesus has set you free!
The stone had been rolled way.
The stone had been rolled away.
Hallelujah my Jesus reigns
Hallelujah my Jesus reigns.
End

-Those who wait on you Jesus, shall never be put shame:

Hallelujah, *I praise oh Lord, oh Lord, I praise you.*
I praise oh Lord, you really have done it for me.
I waited on you Jesus, and now it has paid me
My waiting on you, it really has paid me.
Chorus) Hallelujah, I praise oh Lord, oh Lord, I praise you.
I praise you oh Lord, you really have done it for me.

I waited on you Jesus, and now it has paid me,
You have answered me, so, let me dance for you.
Chorus) Hallelujah, I praise you oh Lord, I praise you.
I praise you oh Lord, you really have done for me.

Those who wait on you Jesus, shall never be put to shame.
Those who trust in you, shall never be put to shame.
Chorus) Hallelujah, I praise oh Lord, oh Lord, I praise you.
I praise oh Lord, you really have done for me.
End.

For His wonders and miracles, I, want to give thanks to the Lord:

Come and go with me, come and go with me.
Come and go with me, come and go with me.
I want to give thanks to the Lord.
I want to give thanks to the Lord.

For all He has done, for all He has done.
I want to give thanks to the Lord.
I want to give thanks to the Lord.

For His wonders and miracles, for His wonders and miracles.
For His mighty power, for His mighty power.
I want to give thanks to the Lord.
I want to give thanks to the Lord.

The Lord is so good, the Lord is so good.
The Lord is so beautiful, the Lord is so beautiful.
I want to give thanks to the Lord.
I want to give thanks to the Lord.

He fought all my battles, He fought all my battles.
He won all my battles, He won all my battles.
I want to give thanks to the Lord.
I want to give thanks to the Lord.
End.

No wonder we call you God, who can understand your ways:

Undefeatable God on my side!

- No wonder we call you God, Jesus, no wonder we call you God!
And you are God on my side,
Who can understand your ways!
Undefeatable God on my side, Jesus,
who can understand your ways!

I got a pen and a paper to write something about you, Jesus,
But I couldn't write anything because I don't know what to say!
Jesus, who can understand your ways!

And you are God on my side,
Undefeatable God on my side,
Who can understand your ways!

Who knows how you will make a way in the wilderness!
Who knows how you bring rivers in the desert!
Who knows how you made a way in red Sea!
Jesus, who can understand your ways!

And you are God on my side,
Undefeatable God on my side,
Who can understand your ways!

How can a small stone hit a that big giant Goliath kill him?
Who can understand how a young Shepherd boy killed a giant?
Jesus, who can understand your ways!

And you are God on my side,
Undefeatable God on my side,
Who can understand your ways!

How can a Shepherd boy kill a lion with his hands?
Jesus, who can understand your ways!
How can a Shepherd kill a bear with his hands?
Jesus, who can understand your ways!

And you Are God on my side,
Undefeatable God on my side,
Who can understand your ways!

Who can understand how Daniel became friendly with Hungry lions over night?
Jesus, who can understand your ways!
And you are God on my side,
Undefeatable God on my side,
Who can understand your way!
End.

I **know who you are Abba Father**, **I, know who you are my Jesus**:

I know who you are oh, my Jesus,
I know who you are Abba Father,
I know who you are oh, my Jesus.
I know who you are oh, oho, oh.

You are a mighty, mighty healer,
You are a mighty deliverer.
Strong in battle oh, oh,
You have never lost any battle.
Oh, my Jesus, I know who you are, (chorus)
I know who you are, Abba Father.
I know who you are, oh, oh, Oh.

You are makes the lame to walk,
You are the one makes the deaf to hear.
You are the one makes blind to see.
You are the one I love Jesus.

Chorus) oh, my Jesus, I know who you are,
I know who you are, Abba Father.
I know who you are, oh, oh.

You are the one brings the dead back to life.
You are the makes the dump to speak.
You are the one mend a broken heart.
You are the one I love Jesus.

Chorus) oh, my Jesus, I know who you are,
I know who you are, Abba Father.
I know who you are, oh, oh, oh.

You are the one says yes, and nobody can say no, no.
You are the one says no, and nobody can say yes.
You are the one opens the door Jesus, and nobody can shut it.
You are the shuts the door Jesus, and nobody can open it.

Chorus) oh, my Jesus, I know who are.
I know who you are, Abba Father.
I know who you are, oh, oh.
End.

My sold rock where I, stand, you *are* beautiful to me:

-Jesus who died for me, my hiding place.
My sold rock where I stand, I give you glory and honour.

You are beautiful to me.
You are beautiful to me.
You Are beautiful to me.
I sing holy, holy to the Lamb.
I sing holy, holy to the Lamb.

Angels bow before you, angels bow before you.
They sing holy, holy to the Lamb.
They sing holy, holy to the Lamb.

I join heavenly angels, I join heavenly angels.
To sing holy, holy to the Lamb.
To sing holy, holy to the Lamb.

Oh Jesus, you are Awesome, Jesus, you are Awesome. Oh Jesus, you are Awesome,
I sing holy, holy to the Lamb.
I sing holy, holy to the Lamb.
End.

I Say thank you Jesus from the bottom of my heart:

I say thank you Jesus, I say thank you Jesus. I say thank you Jesus,
From the bottom of my heart.
From the bottom of my heart.
I praise, I praise you Jesus, I praise, I praise you Jesus.
I praise, I praise you Jesus,
With all my heart, I praise you.
With all my heart, I praise you.

For all you have done for me, for all, you have done for me.
For all you have done for me.
I will praise you forever more.
I will praise you forever more.
Your hand, has given me victory, hallelujah.
Your hand, has given me victory, hallelujah.
I say, thank you Jesus.
From the bottom of my heart.
From the bottom of my heart.
End.

Awesome God, you are winner every day:

Awesome God Jesus, Awesome God. (Chorus)
Awesome God, you are winner every day.
Awesome God, you are a winner every day.
I depend on you Jesus,
I rely on you, my hopes in you every day.
Because I know, Jesus, you will never fail.
Because I know, Jesus, you never lose.

Chorus) Awesome God Jesus, Awesome God.
Awesome God,you are a winner every day.
Awesome God, you are a winner every day.

It is impossible for you to lose Jesus.
It is impossible for you to fail Jesus.
I bless your name, I bless your name, Mighty warrior, Mighty Man in battle.
I praise your name, I praise your name, Mighty warrior, Mighty Man in battle.

Chorus) Awesome God Jesus, Awesome God.
Awesome God, you are a winner every day.
Awesome God, you are a winner every day.
End.

I will bless you Lord, all the time, I will think of your power:

Lord I sing you are holy:

I will bless you, I will bless you Lord.
I will bless you, I will bless you Lord,
All the time, I will think of your goodness, I will think of your power.
All the time, I will think of your greatness.

Because I know Jesus, nothing is impossible for you.
It is impossible for you to lie, it is impossible for to lie to me!
All Sufficient God, you supply all my needs.
You daily load me with benefits, I will bless you all the time.
Oh Jesus, I will bless you, I will bless you Lord.
All the time, I will think of your goodness, I will think of your power.
All the time, I will think of your greatness.
End.

You are my navigator, the driver of music life:

King of glory, the Prince of Peace.
My Redeemer, I worship you.
Mighty in battle, the Strong deliverer.
My Redeemer, I worship you.

The Greater warrior, always a winner.
My Redeemer, I worship you.
Jesus, you are my navigator, the driver of my life.
My Redeemer, I worship you.

You are my tower, my shelter, my hiding place.
My Redeemer, I worship you.

Consuming fire, loving and patient.
My Redeemer, I worship you.
King of glory, the Prince of peace.
My Redeemer, I worship you.
End.

I, know one God I, have, the only God I, know.

I have no other helper:

I know one God I have, I know one God I have. (Chorus)
The only God, I know,
His name is Jesus, He's dressed in majesty
He's dressed in majesty, He's dressed in majesty.
I have no other God, beside you, beside you Jesus.
I have no other God, beside you Jesus.
I have no other helper, beside you, beside you Jesus.
I have no other helper, beside you Jesus.

My help comes from you alone, Jesus.
I have no other helper, beside you Jesus.
I have no other helper, beside you Jesus.

Chorus) I know one God I have, the only God I know.
His name is Jesus, He's dressed in majesty.
He's dressed in majesty, He's in majesty.
End.

God of everything, your name is Adonai:

God of everything, God of everything, God of everything.
Your name is Adonai, your name is Adonai.

I give you all the glory, I give you all the honour, I give you all the praises.
Your name is Adonai, your name is Adonai.

You are not a liar, you are not a loser, you are not a late comer, Jesus.
Your name is Adonai, your name is Adonai.

God of everything, God of everything, God of everything.
Your name is Adonai, your name is Adonai.
End.

Have you ever heard of someone called Jesus?

Do you know my Father? Do you know my Father? Do you know my Father?
Have you ever heard of someone called Jesus?
Have you ever heard of someone called Jesus?
He is God Almighty, He is King of Kings.
He is Lord of lords, He is Alpha and Omega.
He is so Powerful, He is so loving,
He is so wonderful, He has the whole world in His hand.

He gives beauty of ashes, the oil of joy for mourning,
He gives hope to the hopeless, the defender of widows.

He is Father to the fatherless, He mends a broken heart.
He sets the prisoners free, Holy and Awesome is His name.

Do you know my Father? Do you know my Father?
Do you know my Father? Have you ever heard of someone called Jesus?
Have you ever heard of someone called Jesus?
End.

Beginning and End worship you:

Beginning and End, I worship you.
Beginning and End, I worship you.
Beginning and End.
Beginning and End.
Beginning and End.
Beginning and End, I worship you.

God Almighty, I worship you.
Lion of Judah, I worship you.
Beginning and End.
Beginning and End.
Beginning and End, I worship you.

I fall at your feet Jesus, I fall at your feet Jesus.
I bow and worship you.
Oh, I bow and worship you, Beginning and End.
Beginning and End.
Beginning and End, I worship you.

You are powerful and Mighty, you are powerful and Mighty.
Beginning and End.
Beginning and End.
Beginning and End, I worship you.

You are lifted higher Jesus, you are lifted higher Jesus.
Beginning and End.
Beginning and End.
Beginning and End, I worship you.
End.

Your name is wonderful,

King of all kings, I worship you.
King of all kings, I washing you.

King of all kings I love you.
Your name is Wonderful.

Gracious King only you seats, only you seated higher above.
You rule by power and might.
There is no king like you.
King of all kings, I worship you.

Your throne is in heaven, your throne is in heaven.
You rule by power and might, Jesus.
Who can compare with you?
King of all kings, I worship you.
End.

I just want to bless your holy name:

I *just want to bless your holy name, I just want to bless your name.*
I just want to bless your holy name.

Jesus, King of Kings, Saviour, Redeemer, Creator.
I just want to bless your holy name.

Invisible God, Immortal God, Consuming fire, you are full of glory.
I just want to bless your holy name.
End.

Jesus you are the Lamp shining more than all stars of heaven:

Jesus you are the Lamp, Jesus you the Lamp.
Jesus you are the Lamp.
You are the Lamp, shining more that all stars of heaven.
You are the Lamp, shining more than all stars of heaven.

I want to behold your beauty,
I want to behold your beauty.
You are the Lamp, shining more than all stars of heaven.
You Are the Lamp, shining more than all stars of heaven.

I want to behold your glory.
I want to behold your glory.
You are the Lamp, shining more than all stars of heaven.
You are the Lamp, shining more than all stars of heaven.

You are so, so, radiant, you are so, so radiant,
You are so, so, radiant, Jesus, no word can explain it!
You are so, so, radiant, Jesus, no word can explain it.
You the Lamp shining more than all stars of heaven.
End.

Lily of the valley you are so beautiful:

Oh my God, you are so beautiful
Oh my God, you are so beautiful.
You are so beautiful, you are so beautiful.
I tell you, you are so beautiful.
I tell you, you are so beautiful.

Oh Jesus, you are so beautiful.
Oh Jesus, you are so beautiful.
Oh Jesus, you are so beautiful.
I tell you, you are so beautiful.
I tell you, you are so beautiful.

Lily of the valley, you are so beautiful.
Rose of Sharon, you are so beautiful.
You are so real, you are so beautiful.
You are so real, you are so beautiful.
I tell you, you are so beautiful.
I tell you, you are beautiful.

Lion of Judah, you are so beautiful.
What you say, is so beautiful.
What you do, is so beautiful.
I tell you, you are so beautiful.
I tell you, you are doing beautiful.

Elohim, you are so beautiful.
Adonai, you are so beautiful.
You are so radiant, you are so beautiful.
You are so radiant, you are so beautiful.
You are so radiant, you are so beautiful.
I tell you, you are so beautiful.
I tell you, you are so beautiful.

BABA, you are so beautiful.
BABA, you are so beautiful.
BABA, you are so beautiful.
I tell you, you are so beautiful.
I tell you, you are beautiful.

Oh Jesus, you are so beautiful.
Oh Jesus, you are beautiful.
Oh Jesus, you are beautiful.
End.

Among other gods, you are the only living God:

You are my Jesus, you are my Jesus.
You are my Jesus, I will worship you.
You are my Jesus, you are my Jesus.
You are my Jesus, I will worship you.

Forever more, forever more, forever more,
Forever more, forever more, forever more.
You are my Jesus, I will worship you.
You are my Jesus, I will worship you.

Lily of the valley, I will worship you.
Rose of Sharon, I will worship you.
I AM THAT I AM, I will worship you.

Chorus) You are my Jesus, I will worship you.
You are my Jesus, I will worship you.
You are my Jesus, I will worship you.

Impossible doer, I will worship you.
Sovereign God, I will worship you.
Your Highness, I will worship you.

Chorus) you are my Jesus, I will worship you.
You are my Jesus, I will worship you.
You are my Jesus, I will worship you.

Magnificent God, I worship you.
Oh, oh, I will worship you.
King of kings, I will worship you.

Chorus) you are my Jesus, I will worship you.
You are my Jesus, I will worship you.
You are my Jesus, I will worship you.

I salute you, Lord of lords, You are my Jesus, I worship you.
I bow for you, King of kings, you are my Jesus, I will worship you.
I give you honour, oh, oh, oh, you are my Jesus, I will worship you.

Among other gods, You are the only living God.
Among other gods, you are the only living God.

Chorus) you are my Jesus, I will worship you.
You are my Jesus, I will worship you.
You are my Jesus, I will worship you.
End.

With a mighty hand, you brought Israel out of Egypt:

Sovereign God, Sovereign God, Sovereign God, I worship you.
Sovereign God, Sovereign God, Sovereign God, I worship you.

You are God Almighty, you are the God Almighty,
You are the God Almighty, Sovereign God, I worship you.

With your mighty hand, with your hand,
You brought Israel out of Egypt.

You brought Israel out of Egypt.
Sovereign God, I worship you.
End.

You are the fire that burns in water, who can battle with you:

You reign in majesty Man on of war.
You reign in majesty Man of war.
You reign in majesty Man of war.
Who can battle with you? Jesus.
Who can battle with you? Jesus.

You are the fire that burns in water!
You are the fire that burns in water!
You are the fire that burns in water!
Who can battle with you? Jesus.
Who can battle with you? Jesus.
End.

I know why you created me, You created me to worship you:

I know why you created me, Jehovah, I know why you created me.
I know why you created me, Jehovah, I know why you created me.

You created me to worship you.
You created me to worship you.
You created me to worship you.
You created me to worship you.

To bow down for you Jesus.
To bow down for you, oho ho....
To bow down for you Jesus.
You created me to worship you.
You created me to worship you.

I will worship you, yes, I will.
I will worship you, yes, I will.

I will worship you, yes, I will.
You created me to worship you.
You created me to worship you.

To give you all the glory Jesus.
To give you all the glory, oh oho....
To give you all the glory Jesus.
You created me to worship you.
You created me to worship you.

To sing all your praises Jesus.
To sing all your praises, oh ho.....
To sing all your praises Jesus.
You created me to worship you.
You created me to worship you.

To give you all the honour Jesus.
To give you all the honour, oh ho.....
To give you all the honour Jesus.
You created me to worship you.
You created me to worship you.
Elohim, you created me to worship you.
Adonai, you created me to worship you.
You created me to worship you.
You created me to worship you.
End.

Big and Mighty, ***1***

1 ***John 4: 4,***

Greater is He that is in me.
Greater is He that is in me.
Greater is that is in me.

He's Big and Mighty, He's Big and Mighty, Greater is He that is me.
I cannot be defeated, I cannot be defeated, Greater is He that is me.

I have overcome them, I have overcome them, Greater is that is in me.
The one who is in this world is nothing, Greater is He is that in me.
There is nothing good about him, Greater is He that is me.
Greater is He that is me.
End.

When you are with Jesus, Nothing is impossible:

When you with Jesus, nothing is impossible for you to do.
When you are with Jesus, nothing is impossible for you to do.

You can move a mountain, you can move a mountain,
You can move a mountain, when you are with Jesus.
You can walk on water, you can walk on water,
You can walk on water, when you are with Jesus.

You can heal the sick, you can heal the sick.
You can heal the sick, when you are with Jesus.

When you are with Jesus, nothing is impossible for you to do.
Nothing is impossible for you to do.
End.

The hand that touched is so beautiful:

The hand of Jesus, will touch you today.
The hand of Jesus, will touch you today.
Feel the touch of Jesus, feel the touch of Jesus
Feel the touch of Jesus, the touch is permanent

The touch is permanent, the touch is permanent
The hand that touched me, is so beautiful.
The hand that touched me, is so beautiful.
The hand that touched me, is so beautiful.

I will never be the same again, I will never be the same again.
Jesus' hand touched me.
Jesus' hand, Jesus' hand touched me.

I felt a different a touch, I felt a different touch.
Jesus' hand touched me.
Jesus' hand, Jesus' hand touched me.

It was just one touch, Just one touch like this, that I need from Jesus.
It was just one touch, one touch like this, that I needed from Jesus.
Jesus' hand touched me.
Jesus' hand, Jesus' hand touched me.
End.

Jesus you are a wonder, who can deny it?

You are a wonder, oh, Jesus, you are a wonder. (chorus)
You are a wonder Jesus, who can deny it?
You are a wonder Jesus, which can deny it?

I will praise you, I will adore you,
I will lift higher, you are a wonder.
I worship you, I will honour you,
I will bless you Jesus, you are a wonder.

Chorus) you are a wonder, oh, Jesus, you are a wonder.

You are a wonder Jesus, who can deny it?
You are a wonder Jesus, who can deny it?

Jehovah Elushadai, you are wonder.
Adonai, you are a wonder.
Jehovah over giver, you are wonder.
Jehovah over do, you are a wonder.

Chorus) you are a wonder, oh, Jesus, you are a wonder.
You are a wonder Jesus, who can deny it?
You are a wonder Jesus, who can deny it?

In my ministry Jesus, you are a wonder.
In my home Jesus, you are a wonder.

In my family Jesus, you are a wonder.
In my business Jesus, you are a wonder.
In my children Jesus, you are a wonder.

Chorus) you are a wonder, Oh, Jesus, you a wonder.
You are a wonder Jesus, who can deny it?
You are a wonder Jesus, who can deny it?

You have blessed me Jesus, with many blessings,
Uncountable blessings, who can deny it?
You have opened many doors for me, you are a wonder.
You have lifted me higher, who can deny it?

Chorus) you are a wonder, oh, Jesus, you are wonder.
You are a wonder Jesus, who can deny it?
You are a wonder Jesus, who can deny it?
End.

Your name is I AM THAT I AM forever:

I AM THAT I AM, we praise you every day.
That is your name forever, we praise you every day.
I AM THAT I AM, we thank you every day.
That is your name forever, we thank you every day.
I AM THAT I AM, we bless you every day.
That is your name forever, we bless you every day
I AM THAT I AM we love you every day.
That is your name forever, we love you every day.

Lion of Judah, Lion of Judah, your name is I AM THAT I AM forever.
Lion of Judah, Lion of Judah, your name is I AM THAT I AM forever.
I have come to worship you Jesus.
I have come to bow for you Jesus.
I have to salute you Jesus.
Your name is I AM THAT I AM forever.
Your name is I AM THAT I AM forever

You answer by fire, you heal by power, you deliver by power.
Your name is I AM THAT I AM forever.
Your name is I AM THAT I AM forever.

God of Abraham, God of Isaac, God Jacob.
Your name is I AM THAT I AM forever.
Your name is I AM THAT I AM forever.

God of Elijah, God of David, God of Moses.
Your name is I AM THAT I AM forever.
Your name is I AM THAT I AM forever.
God of Daniel, God of Shadrack, God of Meshach and Abednego.
Your name is I AM THAT I AM forever.
Your name is I AM THAT I AM forever.

Lion of Judah, Lion of Judah, your name is I AM THAT I AM forever.
Your name is I AM THAT I AM forever.
End.

Father look at me, can you see how much I adore you?

I humbly worship you Jesus, I humbly worship you.
I humbly worship you Jesus, I humbly worship you.
My heart, magnifies you.
My heart, magnifies you.

I bow in humble adoration,
I bow in humble adoration,
I bow in humble adoration.
Father, can you see how much I adore you?
Father, can you see how much I adore you?
Can you see? Can you see Father ?
Can you see how much I adore you?
Father look at me, Father look at me,
Can you see how much I adore you?
Can you see? Can you see Father?
Can you see how much I adore you?

I humbly worship you Jesus, I humbly worship you.
I humbly worship you Jesus, I humbly worship you.
My heart, magnifies you.
My heart, magnifies you.
End.

Jesus is yearning for our worship:

I step in Jesus, I step in Jesus.
I step in Jesus, I'm available to worship you.
Jesus, I'm available, Jesus, I'm available.
Jesus, I'm available, I'm available to worship you.

From the rising of the sun, from the rising of the sun.
To its going down, Jesus I will worship you.
Jesus, I will worship you.

Come on join me, come on, join me.
(chorus) Come on join me, to worship our God
Come on join me, to worship our God.

Who will worship our God?
Who will worship our God?
Who will worship Him?
Who will worship Him?
Who will worship Jesus?

Jesus is yearning for our worship.
Jesus is yearning for our worship.
He is sitting at the well, He is waiting for who will worship Him.
He is sitting at the well, He is waiting for who will worship Him.

Chorus) come on join me, come on join me.
Come on join me, to worship our God.
Come on join me, to worship our God.

Jesus is thirsty, Jesus is thirsty,
He is sitting at the well, He is waiting for who will worship Him.
Give Jesus a drink, give Jesus a drink,
He is waiting for who will worship Him.
His is waiting for who will worship Him.
Who will worship Him ?
Who will worship Him?
Who will worship Jesus?
Chorus) come on join me, come on join me,
Come on join me, to worship our God.
Come on join me, to worship our God.
End.

I **join heavenly choir to worship:**

You are holy, you are holy, you are holy Awesome Jesus. (Chorus)
You are holy, you are holy, you are holy Awesome Jesus.

I bow and worship, I bow and worship, I bow and worship Jesus.
I join heavenly choir to worship you.
You are holy Awesome Jesus
You are holy Awesome Jesus.

Chorus) you are holy, you are holy, you are holy Awesome Jesus.
You are holy, you are holy, you are holy Awesome Jesus.

God Almighty, Alpha and Omega.
Beginning and End, I worship you.
You are the only King who will reign forever,
You are holy Awesome Jesus.
You are beautiful, you are Mighty,
You so glorious King of kings.

I cry in worship, I cry in worship.
I sing hosanna to the Lamb of God.
I sing hosanna to the Lamb of God.

Chorus) you are holy, you are holy, you are holy Awesome Jesus.
You are holy, you are holy, you are holy Awesome Jesus.
End.

Your Majesty Jesus, we salute you:

The king of kings is in this place,
Bow down and worship Him.
The King of kings is in this place,
Bow down and worship Him.
Your Majesty Jesus,
Your Majesty Jesus.
Most Honourable, we salute you.
Most Honourable, we salute you.

You reign on high Jesus. (chorus)
You reign on high Jesus.
You reign on high Jesus, you are higher than heaven.
You reign on high Jesus, you are higher than heaven.

Glorious King, Glorious King.
The only one who will reign forever.
The only one who will reign forever.
I just want to bow before your throne.
I just want to bow before your throne.
As the angles worship you Jesus.
As the angels worship you.
As the angels worship you.
I wanna be included.
I wanna be included.
Chorus) you reign on high Jesus.
You reign on high Jesus.
You are higher than heaven.
You are higher than heaven.

Heaven and earth shall pass away.
Heaven and earth shall pass away Jesus,
Heaven and earth shall pass away.
But you King of kings shall reign forever more But you King of kings shall reign forever more.
I lay myself at your feet.
I lay myself at your feet.
"cause I was born to worship you.
"cause I was born to worship you.
Chorus) you reign on high Jesus,
You reign on high Jesus.
You are higher than heaven.
You are higher than heaven.

I wanna be number one to worship you.
I wanna be number one to worship you.
So let me pour my praises on to you.
So let me pour my praises on to you.
Chorus) you reign on high Jesus.
You reign on high Jesus.
You are higher than heaven.
You are higher than heaven.
End.

Who I am I, to worship you? Who I am I, to stand in your presence?

My lord and my Saviour.
My Lord and my Saviour.
My Lord and my Saviour.
You are so precious
You are so precious.

It's an honour, it's an honour.
To stand in your presence and worship you.
It's an honour, it's an honour.
To stand in your presence and worship you.

Who I am I, to worship you Jesus?
Who I am I, to worship you?
Who I am I, to worship you?
Who I am I, to worship you?

Who I am I, to worship you Mighty God?
Who I am I, to worship you?
Who I am I, to worship you?
Who I am I, to worship you?
Who I am I, to worship you King of kings?
Who I am I, to worship you?
Who I am I, to worship you? Who I am I, to worship you?

To stand in your presence, who I am I, to worship you?
To bow down for you Jesus, who I am I to worship you?

You dressed in Majesty Jesus,
Clothed in honour,
Who I am I, to worship you?
Who I am I, to worship you?
My Lord and my Savour, you are so precious.
End.

I can't get enough of you, I **will worship you:**

Jehovah Elushadai, Jehovah Elushadai,
Jesus, I will worship you.
Oh, I will worship you.
Oh, Jesus, I can't get enough of you.
I can't get enough of you,
I can't get enough of you,
I will worship you,
I will worship you.

With all my all my heart Jesus,
With all my all my mouth Jesus,
With all my head Jesus.

I will worship you.
Oh, I will worship you.
Oh, Jesus, I can't get enough of you.
I can't get enough of you.
I will worship you, I will worship you.

With all my hands Jesus,
With all my arms Jesus,
With all my fingers Jesus.
I will worship you.
Oh, I will worship you.
Oh, Jesus, I can't get enough you.
I can't get enough for you.
I will worship you,
I will worship you.

With my back Jesus,
With all my hips Jesus,
With my waist Jesus.
I will worship you.
Oh, I will worship you.
Oh, Jesus, I can't get enough of you.
I can't get enough of you.
I will worship you, I will worship you.
With all my legs Jesus,
With all my feet Jesus,
With all my toes Jesus.
I will worship you.
Oh, I will warship you.
Oh, Jesus, I can't get enough of you.
I can't get enough of you.
I will worship you, I will worship you.
Jehovah Elushadai, I will worship you.
End.

I give you praise Mighty God, Mighty to heal, I give you praise:

I give you praise, I give you praise,
I give you praise Mighty God,
I give you praise, Mighty God,

Mighty in battle, Mighty in battle,
Mighty in battle, I give you praise.
Chorus, I give you praise, I give you praise Mighty God.

Mighty to save, Mighty to save.
Mighty to save, I give you praise.
Chorus) I give you praise, I give you Mighty God.

Mighty to deliver, Mighty to deliver.
Mighty to deliver, I give you praise.
Chorus) I give you praise, I give you Praise Mighty God.

Mighty to heal, Mighty to heal.
Mighty to heal, I give you praise.
Chorus) I give you praise, I give you praise Mighty God.
Mighty to answer, Mighty to answer.
Mighty to answer, I give you praise.
Chorus) I give you praise, I give you praise Mighty God.
End.

I lift my voice to worship you, King of kings I worship you:

Great I AM I, worship you,
Great I AM I, worship you.
Great I AM I, worship you,
Jesus, King of kings I worship you.
King of kings I worship you.

I bow before you Great I AM,
I, bow before you Great I AM.
I bow before you Great I AM,

Jesus, King of kings, I worship you.
King of kings, I worship you.

I lift my voice to worship you,
Great I AM, I lift my voice to worship you.
I lift my voice to worship you.
Jesus, King of kings, I worship you.
King of kings, I worship you.

I lift my hands to worship you, Great I AM, I lift my hands to worship you.
I lift my hands to worship you.
Jesus, King of kings, I worship you.
King of kings, I worship you.

I clap my hands to worship you, Great I AM, I clap my hands to worship you.
I clap my hands to worship you.
Jesus, King of kings, I worship you.
King of Kings, I worship you.
I close my eyes to worship you, Great I AM, I close my eyes to worship you.
Jesus, King of kings, I worship you.
King of kings, I worship you.
End.

Majesty, I want to honour you:

Majesty, Majesty, Majesty, (chorus)
Majesty King of kings, I want to honour you.
Majesty King of kings, I want to honour you.

I want to bow and worship you,
I want to bow and worship you.
I want to bow and worship you,
Majesty, I want to honour you.
Majesty, I want to honour you.

I want to give thanks and praise,
I want to give thanks and praise.
I want to give thanks and praise, Majesty,
I want to honour you.
Majesty, I want to honour you.

I want to glorify your name,
I want to glorify your name.
I want to glorify your name.
Majesty, King of kings,
I want honour you.
Majesty, King of kings,
I want to honour you.

Majesty, Majesty, Majesty.
Majesty, King of kings, I want to honour you.
Majesty, King of kings, I want to honour you.
End.

Wherever you go, I want to go, whatever you do, I want to do.

I have come to bow down for you. (chorus)
Kings of kings, I have come to bow down for you,
King of kings, I have come to bow down for you.
Jesus, let me remain in your presence.
Jesus, let me remain in your presence.

Wherever you send me, I want to go.
Whatever you do, I want to do.
Wherever you are, I want to be.
Wherever you go, I want to follow you,
Jesus, let me remain in your presence.
Jesus, let me remain in your presence.
Chorus)

I want to a tree planted in your house.
I want to be a tree planted in house.
Beautiful God, I want to be a tree planted in your house.
Jesus, let me remain in your presence.
Jesus, let me remain in your presence.

Peace and joy are found in your presence.
Strength and hope are found in your presence.
Long life and prosperity are in your presence.
Jesus, let me remain in your presence.
Jesus, let me remain in your presence.

Where can I go from you?
You are the only God I know,
Jesus, let me remain in your presence.
Jesus, Let me remain in your presence.

Where can I go from you?
I have no other God I know, who can love me like you.
I have no other God I know, who can love me like you.
Jesus, let me remain in Your presence.
Jesus, let me remain in your presence.

Where can I go from you?
I have no other God I know, who can heal me like you.
I have no other God I know, who keep me like you.
Jesus, let me remain in your presence.
Jesus, let me remain in your presence.

Where can I go from you?
I have no other God I know, who can help me like you.
I have no other God I know, who can touch me like you.
Jesus, let me remain in your presence.
Jesus, let me remain in your presence.

Where can I go from you?
I have no other God I know, who can save me like you.
I have no other God I know, who can protect me like you.
Jesus, let me remain in your presence.
Jesus, let me remain in your presence.
End.

The name Jesus will never fail:

Give Him glory, give Him honour.
Salute Him, King of kings.
Give Him glory, give Him honour.
Salute Him King of kings.
The name Jesus will never fail, the name Jesus will never fail.
Salute Him King of kings.
Salute Him King of kings.
He is the way, the Truth and Life.
Salute Him King of kings.
Salute Him King of kings.
End

I lift you higher Jesus, you are higher than heave:

Mighty God, I worship you,
Hallelujah, Mighty God, I worship you.
I bow down and worship you.
Oh Lord, you are worthy of my praise.
Oh Lord, you are worthy of my praise.

I lift you higher Jesus,
I lift you higher King of kings.
You are higher than heaven.
Oh Lord, you are worthy of my praise.
Oh Lord, you are worthy of my praise.
End.

When I think of goodness:

When I think of your goodness.
How you made me to be like you.
I cannot think of anything, but to praise your holy name.
But to praise your holy name.

Oh, I will bow, I will bow. (chorus)
I will bow, I will bow.
I will bow and worship you.
I will bow and worship you.

You could have made me to be a goat,
You could have made me to be a cow,
You could have made me to be a chicken,
But you made to be like you.
But you made me to be like you.

Chorus) Oh, I will bow, I will bow.
I will bow, I will bow.
I will bow and worship you.
I will bow and worship you.

You could have me to be a fish,
You could have made to be a buffalo,
You could have made me to be a lion,
But you made me to be like you.
But you made me to be like you.

Chorus) I will bow, I will bow,
I will bow, I will bow,
I will bow and worship you.
I will bow and worship you.
End.

Seated in Majesty, Hassan King of kings:

Your Highness Jesus, your Highness Jesus.
Your Highness Jesus, Great and Majesty.
Your Highness Jesus, Great and Majesty.

Seated in Majesty, Seated in Majesty.
Seated in Majesty, Hassan King of kings.
Seated in Majesty, Hassan King of Kings.
Your Highness Jesus, Great and Majesty.
I bow down and worship you Jesus, I bow down and worship you.
I bow down and worship you, Great and Majesty.
I bow down and worship you, Great and Majesty.

I salute you Jesus, I salute you.
I salute you, Great and Majesty.
I salute you, Great and Majesty.

Your Highness Jesus, Great and Majesty.
Your Highness Jesus, Great and Majesty.
End

You are full of wonders, you are full of surprises:

You are a Great God Jesus, your a Great God.
You are Awesome and wonderful, I lift your name higher.
You are Awesome and wonderful, I lift your name higher.

Awesome God I worship you, Awesome God I worship you.
Awesome God I worship you, Awesome God I worship you.
You are full of wonders, you are full of surprises.
I bless your holy name, I lift you higher.
End.

Oh yaya Baba Jesus, oh yaya Baba Jesus.
Oh yaya Baba Jesus, I praise you, Praise you.
Oh yaya Baba, Jesus, I praise you, I praise you.

Oh yaya Baba Jesus, oh yaya Baba Jesus.
Oh yaya Baba Jesus, I love you, I love you.
Oh yaya Baba Jesus, I love you, I love you
Oh yaya Baba Jesus, oh yaya Baba Jesus.
Oh yaya Baba Jesus, I thank you, I thank you.
Oh yaya Baba Jesus, I thank you, I thank you.

My heart will sing, of your goodness in my life.
My heart will sing, of your goodness in my life,
Jehovah Elushadai, I tell you, you are sooo good to me.
Jehovah Elushadai, I tell you, your are sooo good to me.
End,

Who is worthy of all our worship?

Who is worthy, of all our praises? It's you, it's you, Jesus.
Who is worthy, of all our worship? It's you, it's you, Jesus.
Our healer, our Doctor, our Great physician? It's you, it's you, Jesus.
Our warrior, Mighty Man in battle? It's you, it's you, Jesus.
Our Father, our Saviour? It's you, it's you, Jesus.

Our hiding place, the Strong Tower? It's you, it's you, Jesus.
Lily of the Valley, Great I am? It's you, it's you, Jesus.
Our refuge, our sold rock? It's you, it's you, Jesus.
Our Shepherd, our provider? It's you, it's you, Jesus.
Our peace, our comforter? It's you, it's you, Jesus.
Our navigator, our controller? It's you, it's you, Jesus.
Majestic God, dressed in honour? It's you, it's you, Jesus.
Not a loser, always a winner? It's you, it's you, Jesus.
Never a late comers, always on time? It's you, it's you, Jesus.
I said, who is worthy, of all our worship? It's you, it's you, Jesus.
End.

I will sing before you King of kings:

Before your throne, before your throne.
Before your throne, before your throne.
Before your throne, I will bow.
Before your throne, I will bow.
I will bow I will bow, I will bow.
I will bow before you King of kings.
I will before you Lord of lords
I will bow and worship you.
I will bow and worship you.

Before your throne, before your throne.
Before your throne, before your throne.
Before your throne, I will dance.
Before your throne, I will dance.
I will dance, I will dance.
I will dance before you King of kings.
I will dance before your Lord of lords.
I will dance and worship you.
I will dance and worship you.

Before your throne, before your throne.
Before your throne, before your throne.
Before your throne, I will sing. I will sing, I will sing.
I will before you King of kings.
I will sing before you Lord of lords.
I will sing and worship you.
I will sing and worship you.

Before your throne, before your throne.
Before your throne, I will throne.
Before your throne, I will jump.
Before your throne, I will jump.
I will jump, I will Jump.

I will jump before you Kings.
I will jump before you Lord of lords.
I will jump, I will jump.
I will jump and worship you.
I will jump and worship you.

Before your throne, before your throne.
Before your throne, before your throne.
Before your throne, I will clap.
Before your throne, I will clap.
I will clap, I will clap.
I will clap before King of kings.
I will clap before you Lord of lords.
I will clap, I will clap.
I clap and worship you.
I will clap and worship you.
End.

Spirit of the Living God;

Spirit of the Living God, I reverence you.
Spirit of the Living God, I reverence you.
Honourable Jesus, I bow down to worship you.
Honourable Jesus, I bow down to worship you.
End.

With all my being;

With all my being, I fall down at your feet Jesus.
With all my being, I fall down at your feet Jesus.
With all my being, I fall down at your feet to worship you.
With all my being, I fall down at your feet to worship you.

Mighty warrior, I fall down at your feet to worship you.
Rose of Sharon, I fall down at your feet to worship you.

King of glory, I fall down stairs your feet to worship you.
Mighty God, I fall down at your feet to worship you.

With all my being, I fall down at your feet Jesus.
With all my being, I fall down at your feet Jesus.
End.

Master of universe I praise your name;

Precious Jesus, I worship you.
Precious Jesus, I worship you.
Master of universe, I praise your name.
Master of universe I praise your name.

We praise you Alpha, we praise you Omega.
We praise you Alpha, we praise you Omega.
Alpha and Omega Jesus,
Alpha and Omega,
Alpha and Omega, we your holy name.
Alpha and Omega, we bless your holy name.
We bless your holy name.
End.

Precious Great I am, there no is King like you;

We worship you, precious King of glory.
We worship you, Great I am.
We worship you, precious King glory.
We worship you, Great I am.
Precious King of glory.
There is no King like you.
Precious Great I am.
There is no God like you.
And that is why we bow and worship you.
That is why we reverence you.
That is why we salute you,

Precious King of glory, there is no God like you.
Precious Great I am, there is no King like you.
We worship you, Precious King of glory.
We worship you, Great I am.
End.

Let us bow and worship you.

Powerful and Mighty, holy and Awesome.
You are the God who saves.
Let us now and worship you.

Savour of the world, saviour of the world.
Saviour of the world,
Redeemer, every knee must worship you.
Saviour of the world,
Redeemer, every knee must worship you.
End.

Above principalities;

We bow and worship the Lamb who was slain.
Who sits on the throne, who sits higher above.
Above principalities, above principalities.
Seated higher above.
Oh Jesus, we bow and worship you.
End.

You are the Mighty God, you are the Prince of peace;

You are the Mighty God.
You are the Prince of peace.
King of glory, I worship you.
I praise your name, I honour you.
My Great I am, you are my peace.
My Great I am, you are my King.
End.

I will proclaim your Majesty:

You alone are holy.
You alone Jesus are worthy.
You are so faithful and true.
I bless your holy name.
I bless your holy name.
That is I sing and worship you.
That is why I sing and worship you.
To proclaim your Majesty,
You are amazing in my life.

Oh, that is why I sing worship you.
That is why I sing and worship you.
To proclaim your Majesty.
You are amazing in my life.
You are amazing in my life.

You gave my life a meaning,
You showed me the way to go.
You lifted me oh, Jesus.
I will proclaim your Majesty.
Hallelujah, hallelujah,
Hallelujah, hallelujah, Jesus,
I proclaim your Majesty.
I sing hallelujah, hallelujah, Jesus,
I proclaim your Majesty.
End.

The King of glory, who once was dead;
Hallelujah, hallelujah, Hallelujah, Jesus I, worship you.
Hallelujah, hallelujah, hallelujah, Jesus I, worship you.
The King of glory who once was dead.
Seated upon the throne, Jesus I, worship you.

I bow before you, I fall at your feet.
I lay prostate, Jesus to worship you.
The only King holy and Awesome.
Powerful and Mighty, Jesus I, worship you.
Hallelujah, hallelujah,
Hallelujah, Jesus I, worship you.

I fix my eyes on you,
I fix my eyes on you.
The only King seated upon the throne.
I fix my eyes on you,
I fix my eyes on you,
The only King seated higher above.
Hallelujah, hallelujah.
Hallelujah, Jesus I, worship you.
Hallelujah, Hallelujah,
Hallelujah, Jesus I, worship you.
End.

Oh Lord God Almighty, you are holy Jesus;

You are holy, you are holy,
Oh Lord God Almighty,
You are holy, you are holy,
You are holy Jesus.

You are precious, you are precious.
Oh Lord God Almighty.
You precious, you are precious.
You are precious Jesus.

You are beautiful, you are so' beautiful.
Oh Lord God Almighty.
You are beautiful, you are beautiful.
You are beautiful Jesus.

You are Awesome, you are Awesome.
Oh Lord God Almighty.
You are Awesome, you are Awesome.
You are Awesome Jesus.

You are wonderful, you are wonderful.
Oh Lord God Almighty.
You are wonderful, you are wonderful.
You are wonderful Jesus.

There is a song in my heart to sing;

Melody, oh melody, there is a song in my heart to sing.
Melody, oh Melody, there is a song in my heart to sing.
I'm singing, I'm singing, I'm singing for Jesus.
I'm dancing, I'm dancing, I'm dancing for King of kings.
I'm jumping, I'm jumping, I'm jumping for Jesus.
I have a reason to dance,
I have a reason to praise my God.
He is so Good, He's so good to me.
Melody, oh Melody there is a song in my heart to sing.
End.

Lion of Judah, we glorify you;

We glorify you, we glorify you.
We glorify you, we glorify.
Lion of Judah, we glorify you.
We glorify you.

Consuming fire, we worship you.
Consuming fire, we worship you,
End.

I see everything in a new light:

Glorious King, you are so radiant,
Glorious King, you are so radiant.

You light my ways, Jesus, you light my ways
You light my ways, Jesus, You light my ways,
I see everything in a new light Jesus.
I see everything in a new light Jesus.

You are brighter than a sunny day.
You are brighter than a shining star.
You are so beautiful, to behold Jesus.
You are so beautiful, to behold Jesus.
You light my ways, Jesus, you light my ways.
You light my ways, Jesus, you light my ways.
I see everything in a new light Jesus.
I see I see everything in a new light Jesus.
You are more beautiful than a crystal glass.
You are more beautiful than the precious stone.
You are so beautiful to behold Jesus.
You are so beautiful to behold Jesus.
You light my ways, Jesus, you light my ways.
You light my ways, Jesus, you light my ways.
I see everything in a new light Jesus.
I see everything in a new light Jesus.
End.

All creation bow and worship you:

You are, you are, you are Jesus,
You are, you are, you are Jesus.
You are, you are, you are Jesus.
You are holy and Mighty
You are holy and Might.

All creation, now and worship you.
All creation, bow and worship you.
For who you are, for who you are Jesus.
For who you are, for who you are Jesus.

You are holy and Mighty.
You are holy and Mighty.
End.

Covenant keeping God:

I worship you Covenant keeping God,
Jehovah, Covenant keeping God, I worship you.
Covenant keeping God, I worship you.
Jehovah, Covenant keeping God, I worship you.
You will never, never change, I worship you.
Jehovah, Covenant keeping God, I worship you.
You will never, never lie, I worship you.
Jehovah, Covenant keeping God, I worship you.
You will never, never lose, I worship you.
Jehovah, Covenant keeping God I worship you.

God of Abraham, I worship you.
God of Isaac, I worship you.
You are the God of Jacob, I worship you.
Jehovah, Covenant keeping God, I worship you.
Jehovah, Covenant keeping God, I worship you.
End.

Holy spirit come upon me:

Thank you Holy spirit for giving Isaiah such a song:

My son wrote this song in 2018, I'm borrowing it!

Holy spirit, you are welcome, fill this temple, Hallelujah.
Holy spirit, you are welcome, fill this temple, Hallelujah.
Holy spirit, come upon me, fill this temple, Hallelujah.
Holy spirit, come upon me, fill this temperature, Hallelujah.
I will exact you, I will exalt you, forever and ever, I will exalt you.
I will exalt you, I will exalt you, forever and ever, I will exalt you.

For you are mine, and I'm yours, I will exalt you.
For you are mine and I'm yours, I will exalt you.
For you are mine and I'm yours, I will exalt you.
For you are mine and I'm yours, I will exalt you.
End.

Thank you holy spirit for giving Isaiah such a song.

It's going to rain today:

Can you hear the sound of rain?
Can you hear, the sound of rain?
Can you hear, the sound of rain?
It's gonna rain today, it's gonna rain today.
It's gonna rain today, it's gonna rain today,
It's gonna rain today.

In this rain I do not need umbrella.
In this rain I do not need umbrella.
In this rain I do not need umbrella.
Let it fall on me, let it fall on me, (you)
Let it fall on me, let it fall on me, (you)
You must be so wet.
You must be so wet.

It is raining, it is raining,
Showers from Jesus, are falling down.
Showers from Jesus, are falling down.
Showers from Jesus, are wetting me, (you)
Showers from Jesus, are wetting me, (you)
Showers of healing are falling down.
Showers of healing are falling down.
End.

Once upon a time when my son was in year six, I wanted to buy a pair new school shoes for him, but I was struggling. I said if I buy a shoe then we will have enough money to live on! I was looking for a **cheap shoe** but his foot had grown! Targeting sales but I couldn't wait for sales any more! I said how can I buy a shoe on full price?! I found a pair but it was expensive. Final I decided to buy it. I paid for the shoes and he carried it, as soon we came out of the shop just in town, I saw/heard him singing a song but I had never heard it before! I like it the message in the song, it was touching, so I asked him, where did you hear this song? He answered, I just heard right now, I got it from heaven right now. God was telling that money comes from heaven. Don't worry mummy your money is coming from above, you will not struggle to buy shoes for me again! *Blessing coming from above.*

Blessings coming from above:

All day every day, blessing coming from above.
All day every day, blessings coming from above.
All day every day, healing coming from above.
All day every day, healing coming from above.
All day every day, money coming from above.
All day every day, money coming from above.
End.

Thank spirit of God for giving Isaiah this song!

Jesus is walking in our midst today:

Today, today, is your day of miracle.
Today, today, is your day of miracles.
I have come to tell you that, today, is your day of miracle.
I have come to tell you that, today, is your day of miracles.
You have had enough of everything I know.
You have had enough of everything I know.
How do I know that today is your of miracles.
Because Jesus, around, because Jesus is around.

Today, is your day of miracle.
There is a miracles, oh there is a miracle.
Oh there is a miracle here today.

There is a miracle, oh there is a miracle.
There is a miracle here today.
Jesus is walking, in our midst today.
Jesus is walking, in our midst today.
Jesus is moving among us today.
There is a miracle here today.
A miracles, bow and worship Him.
Oh, bow and worship Jesus.
There is a miracle here today.
There is a miracle here today.
End.

God Almighty, I worship you;

The Most High God I worship you.
I bow on my knees and worship you.
I bow on my knees and worship you.
God Almighty, I worship you.

You, who have done us great things.
Oh Lord, who is like you?
Oh Lord, who is like you?
The Most High God I worship you.
I bow on my knees and worship you.
I bow on my knees and worship you.
God Almighty, I worship you.
God Almighty, I worship you.
End.

Without any doubt:

Without any doubt,
The God I serve is Amazing, is an Awesome God.
Without any doubt,
The God I serve is Amazing, Is an Awesome God.
He's Amazing, is Amazing, is Amazing.

Is Amazing, is an Awesome God.
Without any doubt,
The God I serve is Amazing is an Awesome God.
End.

Alpha and Omega, we thank you very much:

Alpha and Omega, we give you all the glory.
Alpha and Omega, we give you all the honour.
Alpha and Omega, we give all the praises.
Alpha and Omega, we thank you very much.
End.

I declare your glory:

Jehovah Beautiful, Jehovah Beautiful.
I mention your name every day.
I mention your name every day.

Jehovah Elohim, Jehovah Elohim.
I mention your name every day.
I mention your name every day.
Jehovah Powerful, Jehovah Powerful.
I mention your name every day.
I mention your name every day.

I declare your glory, among the nations
I declare your glory, among the nations.
Jehovah Beautiful I mention your name every day.
Jehovah Elohim, I mention your name every day.
Jehovah Powerful, I mention your name every day.
End.

Rock of Ages:

Rock of Ages, we worship you.
Rock of Ages, we worship you.

We praise you, we adore you, we worship you.
We praise you, we adore you, we worship you.
Chorus) Oh, Rock of Ages, we worship you.
Rock of Ages, we worship you.

We worship your holy name, we worship you.
We worship your holy name, we worship you.
Chorus) Oh, Rock of Ages, we worship you.
Rock of Ages, we worship you.

Our God, our God, we worship you.
Our God, our God, we worship you.
Chorus) Oh, Rock of Ages, we worship you.
Rock of Ages, we worship you.
End.

Ancient of days:

Ancient of days, I worship you, for you are worthy of my praise.
Rock of Ages, I worship you, for you are worthy of my praise
You are worthy, you are worthy Jesus.
You are worthy of my praise.
End.

Born to be the King of kings;

We worship you, we worship you.
We bow down and worship you.
We worship you, we worship you.
We bow down and worship.
Born to be the King of kings.
Born to be the King of kings,
Born to be the King of kings.
Immanuel, Immanuel.
Immanuel, Immanuel, King Jesus, we worship you.

We praise you, we adore you.
We love you Most High.
Born to be the King of Kings.
Born to be the King of kings.
Born to be the king of kings.
Immanuel, Immanuel.
Immanuel, Immanuel, King Jesus, we worship you.
End.

The only humble King born in a manger;

There is no on like you, oh Jesus, there is no one.
There is no one, oh Jesus, there is no one like you.
There is no one, oh Jesus, there is no on like you.

You are the only one, Jesus, born of a virgin girl!
You are the only one, Jesus, born of a virgin girl!
There is no one like you, oh Jesus, there is no one.
There is no one, oh Jesus, there is no one like you.
There is no one, oh Jesus, there is one like you.
I have never seen a king, born in a manger!
I have never seen a king, born in mangers!
King of kings, you are the only one, Jesus born in a manger.
You are the only humble King born in a manager.
You are the only humble King born in a manger.
There is no one like you, Oh Jesus, there is one.
There is no one, oh Jesus, there is no one like you.
There is no one, oh Jesus, there is one like you.

I have never seen a Prince, born in a manger!
I have never seen a Prince, born in a manger!
Prince of peace, you are the only one, Jesus, born in a manger.
You are the only humble Prince, born in a manger.
There is no one like you, Oh Jesus, there is no one.
There is no one, oh Jesus, there is no one like you.

There is no one, oh Jesus, there is no one like you.
End

Angels bow and worship Him, they shout hallelujah;

Oh Jesus is worthy, oh my King is worthy,
Jesus is worthy, He's worthy to be praised.
Jesus is worthy, He's worthy to be praised.
Angles bow and worship Him, they shout hallelujah.
They lift Him higher, the Lamb who was slain.

I will bow and worship Him, I will shout hallelujah.
I will lift Him higher, the Lamb who was slain.

Come on bow and worship Him, come on shout hallelujah.
Lift Jesus higher, the Lamb who slain.
Oh Jesus, is worthy, oh my King is worthy.
Jesus is worthy, He's worthy to be praised.
End.

On the cross at Calvary:

Worthy is the Lamb, worthy is the Lamb. ×2
Who takes away the sins of the world.
Who takes away the sins of the world.
You came from heaven because of me.
A friend of sinners, hater of sin.
To die for me to die for you.
Lamb of God, I worship you.
Lamb of God, I worship you.
Chorus) worthy is the Lamb, worthy is the Lamb.
Who takes away the sins of the world.

On the hill Calvary, Lamb of God you went for me.
You were beaten because of me.

Lamb of God I, worship you.
Lamb of I, worship you.
Chorus) worthy is the Lamb, worthy is the Lamb.
Who takes away the sins of the world.
On the hill at Calvary, the Crown of thorns you wore for me.
You were crucified because of me.
Lamb of God I worship you.
Lamb of God, I worship you.
Chorus) worthy is the Lamb, worthy is the Lamb.
Who takes away the sins of the world.

On the hill at Calvary, Lamb of you Bled for me.
Nails in your feet, nails in your hands because of me.
Lamb of God, I worship you.
Lamb of God I worship you.
Chorus) worthy is the Lamb, worthy is the Lamb.
Who takes away the sins of the world.
End.

I was blind and now I see:

Lord I, believe and worship you. (Chorus)
Lord I believe and worship you.
To you alone be the glory.
To you alone be the glory.

You are only God I, know.
You the only God I, know.
Jesus I, will follow you.
I was blind and now I, see.
To you alone be the glory.
To you alone be the glory. Chorus)
End.

Give me a deeper revelation of you:

Give me a deeper revelation of you. (chorus)
Give me a deeper revelation of you.
Give me a deeper revelation of you.
Give me a deeper revelation of you.

Jesus, I Want to see you, I want to see you.
I want to you, Jesus, I want to see you,
Baba, I want to see you.
Give me a deeper revelation of you. Chorus)

Jesus, I want to hear you, I want to hear you.
I want to hear you, Jesus, I want to hear you speak.
Baba, I want to hear you speak.
Give me a deeper revelations of you. Chorus)

Open my eyes, I want to see, open my eyes, I want to see.
Open my eyes I want to see, I want to see you.
Jesus, I want to see you, I want to see you.
Give me a deeper revelation of you. Chorus).

Open my ears I want to hear, open my ears I want to hear.
Jesus, I want to hear you speak, I want to hear you speak.
Give me a deeper revelation of you. Chorus).

Open my heart Jesus, I want to understand.
Open my heart Jesus, I want to understand.
I want to know you, I want to know you.
Baba, I want to know you.
Jesus, I want to know you.
Give me a deeper revelation of you. Chorus)
End.

Increase in me Jesus:

Increase in me Jesus, increase me.
I decrease, Jesus, increase in me.
I decrease, Jesus, increase in me.

Have you way in me Jesus, have your in me.
Oh Jesus, increase in me.
I decrease, Jesus increase in me.
I decrease, Jesus increase in me.

Lay your hands on me Jesus, lay your on me I pay.
Oh Jesus increase in me.
I decrease, Jesus increase in me.
I decrease, Jesus increase in me.
Breathe on me Jesus, breathe on me, I pray. Oh, Jesus increase in me
I decrease, Jesus increase in me.
I decrease, Jesus increase in me.

Shine your light in me Jesus, shine your light in me, I pray.
Oh, Jesus, increase in me.
I decrease, Jesus increase in me.
I decrease, Jesus increase in me.
Let your fire burn in me Jesus, let your fire burn in me, I pray.
Oh, Jesus, increase in me.
I decrease, Jesus increase in me.
I decrease, Jesus increase in me.

Let your power fall on me Jesus, let your power fall on me, I pray.
Oh, Jesus, increase in me.
I decrease, Jesus increase in me.
I decrease, Jesus increase in me.

Let your anointing fall on me Jesus, let your anointing fall on me, I pray
Oh, Jesus, increase in me.

I decrease, Jesus increase in me.
I decrease, Jesus increase in me.

Be my teacher Jesus, be my teacher I, pray.
Oh Jesus, Increase in me.
I decrease, Jesus increase in me.
I decrease, Jesus increase in me.

Be my guide Jesus, be my guide everyday.
Oh Jesus, increase in me.
I decrease, Jesus increase in me.
I decrease, Jesus increase in me.

Be my controller Jesus, be my controller be everyday.
Oh Jesus, increase in me.
I decrease, Jesus increase in me.
I decrease, Jesus, increase in me.
End.

I want to be a flame of fire;

I want to be a burning and shining lamp
I want to be a burning and shinning lamp.
Oh Jesus, have your way in me.
Oh Jesus, have your way in me.

I want to be a burning and shinning light.
I want to a burning and shinning light.
Oh Jesus, have your way in me.
Oh Jesus, have your way in me.

I want to be a flame of fire Jesus.
I want to be a flame of fire Jesus,
Burning hot for you.
Burning hot for you.
Oh Jesus, have your way in me.
On Jesus, have your way in me.

I want to be your hands Jesus.
I want to be your hands Jesus.
Touching lives for you.
Touching lives for you.
Oh Jesus, have your way in me.
Oh Jesus, have your way in me.
I want to be your legs and feet Jesus.
I want to be your legs and feet Jesus.
Running around for you.
Running around for you.
Oh Jesus, have your way in me.
Oh Jesus, have your way in me.
I want to be a burning and shinning lamp.
I want to be a burning and shinning lamp.
Oh Jesus, have your way in me.
Oh Jesus, have your way in me.
End.

As I wait on you Jesus, I will worship you;
(they was a prayer behind this song.)

Jesus I'm waiting on you, Jesus I'm waiting on you.
Jesus I'm waiting on you, Jesus I will wait on you.
As I wait on you Jesus, Jesus as I wait on you.
As I wait on you Jesus, Jesus I will worship you.
I will worship you, Jesus I worship you, as I wait on you.
Because I know Jesus, Jesus because I know.
My calendar is not your calendar.
Because I know Jesus, because I know.
My timing is not your timing.

Jesus I'm waiting on you, Jesus I'm waiting on you.
Jesus I'm waiting on you, Jesus I will wait on you.
As I wait on you Jesus, Jesus as I wait on you.

As I wait on you Jesus, I will praise you.
I will praise you Jesus I will praise you, as I wait on you.
Because I know Jesus, Jesus because I know.
My calendar is not your calendar.
Because I know Jesus, Jesus because I know.
My timing is not your timing.

Jesus I'm waiting on you, Jesus I'm waiting on you.
Jesus I'm waiting on you, Jesus I will wait on you.
As I wait on you Jesus, Jesus as I wait on you.
As I wait on you Jesus, Jesus I will thank you.
I will thank you Jesus I will thank you, as I wait on you.
Because I know Jesus, Jesus because I know November
My calendar is not your calendar.
Because I know Jesus, because I know.
My timing is not your timing.

Jesus I'm waiting on you, Jesus I'm waiting on you.
Jesus I'm waiting on you, Jesus I will wait on you.
As I wait on you Jesus, Jesus as I wait on you.
As I wait on you Jesus, Jesus I will serve you.
I will serve you, Jesus I, will serve you as I wait on you.
Because I know Jesus, because I know.
My calendar is not your calendar.
Because I know Jesus, Jesus because I know.
My timing is not your timing.
Jesus, I'm waiting on you.
End.

I know my Redeemer lives;
(this song was a conversation between me and myself!)

It is well with me, oh yes I know.
It is well with me, I have an assurance.
I tell myself every day, that it is well with me.

I know my Redeemer lives, it is well with me.
I know my Redeemer lives, it is well with me.
Things may be tough at the moment, but it is well with me.
It may be cloudy at the moment but the sun will shine.
I tell myself every day, that it is with me,
I know my Redeemer lives it is well with me.
Oh oh, It is well with me, oh yes I know. It is well with me, I have an assurance.
I tell myself every day, It is well with me.
I know my Redeemer lives, it is well with me.
I know my Redeemer lives, it is well with me.

There may be many challenges, but it is well the me.
Difficult situations after problems, but my tomorrow is glorious.
I tell myself every day, it is well with me.
I know my Redeemer lives, it is well with me.
I know my Redeemer lives, it is well with me.
Oh oh, it is well with me, oh yes I know.
It is well with me, I have an assurance.
It myself every day, it is well with me.
I know my Redeemer lives, it is well with me.
I know my Redeemer lives, it is well with me.
End.

I heard news that made me dance:

This song came to my head after receiving good news concerning UK visa!

I heard news that made me jump, I heard news that made me jump.
I heard news that made me jump.
Settlement has come in my life, settlement has come in my life.

I heard news that made me dance, I heard news that made me dance.
I heard news that made me dance.
Settlement has come in my life, oh, settlement has come in my life.
I heard news that made me sing, I heard news that made me sing.

I heard news that made me sing.
Settlement has come in my life, settlement has come in my life.

My phone rang and I went to pick, my phone rang and I went to pick it.
I heard new that made me jump.
I heard news that made me dance.
I heard news that made me sing.
Settlement has come in my life.
Settlement has come in my life.

I praise you Jesus, I praise you.
I praise you Jesus, I praise you.
I praise you Jesus, I praise you.
Thank you Father, thank you, thank you Jesus for fighting.
Thank you Father, thank you, thank you Jesus for fighting.
Settlements has come in my life.
Settlement has come in my life.

Suffering, I say good bye, worries, I say goodbye bye.
Depression, I say goodbye.
Settlement has come in my life.
Settlement has come in my life.

I waited patient, I waited on God.
With my worship, with my praises.
I waited, I waited on God, at long last He has answered me.
He will never lie, Jesus never lies.
He has answered me, He has answered me.
Settlement has come in my life,
Settlement has come in my life.
One room, I say goodbye, with a child in one room,
One bed, only one bed, one bed, only none bed.
Settlement has come in my life,
Settlement has come in my life.

I would praise Him, I would tell Him.
Jesus, I'm waiting, Jesus I'm waiting on you.
He has answered, He had answered me.
Settlement has come in my life, settlement has come in my life.
End.

There some songs you receive and as you are singing, you feel the story behind that song! Singing this song I was looking at those two legs mountains, as I sang my song I could see them. It was not easy but it was easy with God on my side. When you don't know what to do any more but to only to praise Him.

He surely gave to them, love and justice!

I'm singing a song of victory.

God has dealt with my enemies, God has dealt with my enemies
God has dealt with my enemies.
I'm singing a song of victory, I'm singing a song of victory.
I'm dancing a dance of victory, I'm dancing a dance of victory.
I'm laughing at laugh of victory, I'm laughing a laugh of victory,
I'm jumping a jump of victory, I'm jumping a jump of victory.
I'm shouting a shout of victory, I'm shouting at shout of victory.

God has dealt with my Pharaoh, God has dealt with my Pharaoh.
God has dealt with my Pharaoh.
I'm singing a song of victory, I'm singing a song of victory.
I'm dancing a dance of victory, I'm dancing and dance of victory.
I'm laughing a laugh of victory, I'm laughing a laugh of victory.
I'm jumping a jump of victory, I'm jumping a jump of victory.
I'm shouting a shout of victory, I'm shouting a shout of victory.

God has dealt with my Goliath, God dealt with my Goliath.
God has dealt with my Goliath.
I'm singing a song of victory. I'm singing a song of victory.
I'm dancing a dance of victory, I'm dancing and dance of victory.
I'm laughing at laugh of victory, I'm laughing at laugh of victory.

I'm jumping a jump of victory, I'm jumping a jump of victory.
I'm shouting at shout of victory, I'm shouting a shout of victory.

He has set a table for me before them.
He has anointed my head, now my cup runs over
I'm singing a song of victory, I'm sing a song of victory
I'm dancing and dance of victory, I'm dancing a dance of victory
I'm laughing at laugh of victory, I'm laughing a laugh of victory.
I'm jumping a jump of victory, I'm jumping a jump of victory.
I'm shouting a shout of victory, I'm shouting a shouting of victory.
End.

How beautiful for God to set a table for me before them! And as I eat they are just standing and looking! Because they need to be alive and around to see God's Power over my life. I love them because they pushed and encouraged me to climb higher and higher.

You walk with me in the fire:

Be lifted higher Jesus, be lifted higher Jesus.
Be lifted higher Jesus, higher above, higher Jesus.
Higher above higher Jesus.
Higher above higher Jesus.
There is no other God except you, There is no other God except you.
There is no other God except you, be lifted higher Jesus.
Higher above higher Jesus.
Higher above higher Jesus.

You walk with me in the fire.
You walk with me in the fire.
You walk with in the fire, be lifted higher Jesus.
Higher above higher Jesus.
Higher above higher Jesus.
End.

I was inspired to write this song while reading the book of Daniel, King Nebuchadnezzar and three Hebrew boys, Shadrach, Meshach and Abed-Nego. This king thought he could make these three Hebrew boys who worshipped the only true God to bow for his golden image, small god.

The holy disobedient, *Daniel 3: 8 -28, Therefore at time certain Chaldeans came forward and accused the Jews.*

V9,They spoke and said to King Nebuchadnezzar, "O king live forever.

V10, You O,King have made a decree that everyone who hears the sound of a horn, flute, harp, lyre and psaltery: in symphony with all kinds of music, shall fall and worship the golden image.

V11, And whoever does not fall and worship the golden image shall be cast into the midst of a burning fiery furnace.

V12, There are certain Jews whom you have set over the affairs of the province of Babylon: Shadrack, Meshach and Abed-nego, these me O king have not paid due regard to you, they do not serve your gods or worship the golden image which you have set up.

V13, Then Nebuchadnezzar in rage and fury gave a command to bring Shadrach, Meshach and Abed- nego, so they brought these men before the king.

V14, Nebuchadnezzar spoke say to them, "is it true Shadrach, Meshach and Abed-nego, that you do not serve my gods or worship the golden image which I have set up?

V15, Now if you are ready at the time you hear the sound of the horn, flute, harp, lyre, and psalter you in symphony with all kinds of music fall down and worship the image which I have made good! But if you do not worship, you shall be cast immediately into the midst of a burning fiery furnace and who is that ***god*** *who will deliver you from my hands?*

V16, Shadrach, Meshach and Abed-nego answered, and said to the king, "O Nebuchadnezzar, we no need to answer you in this matter.

V17, If that the case our God whom we serve is able to deliver us from a burning fiery furnace and He will deliver us from your hands, O king.

V18, But if not let it be known to you, O king, that we do not serve your gods, nor will we worship your gold image which you set up."

V19, Then king Nebuchadnezzar was full of fury and expression on his face changed towards Shadrach, Meshach and Abed-nego . Therefore he spoke and commanded that they heat the fiery furnace seven times more that it was usually heated.

V20, And he commanded certain might men of valour who were in the army to bind Shadrach, Meshach and Abed-nego, and cast them into the burning fiery furnace.

V21, Then these men were bound in their coats, their trousers, their turbans and their other garments, and we're cast into the burning fiery furnace.

V22,Therefore because the King's command was urgent and the furnace exceedingly hot, the flame of the fire killed those men who took Shadrach, Meshach and Abed-Nego.

V23, And those three men Shadrach, Meshach, and Abed-Nego, fell down bound into the midst of the burning fiery furnace.

V24, Then King Nebuchadnezzar was astonished: and he rose in haste and spoke, saying to his counsellors, "Did we not cast three men into the midst of the fire? They answered and said, to the king, "True, O king."

V25, Look, He answered, "I see four men loose, walking in the midst fire and they are not hurt, and the form of the ***fourth*** *Man is like the Son of God.*

V26, Then king Nebuchadnezzar, went near the mouth of the burning fiery furnace and spoke saying, "Shadrach, Meshach, and Abed-Nego, servants of the Most High God, come out and come here, then they came from the midst of the fire.

V27, And the satraps administrators, governors and the king's counsellors gathered together and they saw these men on whose bodies the fire had no power, the hair of their heads was not singed nor were their garment affected and the smell of fire was not on them.

V28, Nebuchadnezzar spoke, saying, "Blessed be the God of Shadrach Meshach and Abed-nego, who sent His Angels and delivered His servants who trusted in Him and frustrated the king's words and yielded their bodies that they should not serve nor worship any god except their own God.

But I go back to the same *Daniel 3:* v15, *I see that King Nebuchadnezzar said to the three Hebrew boys, " But if you do not worship my small god, you shall be cast immediately into the midst of a burning furnace, "And who is the* **god** *who will deliver you from my hands?*

And now read same *Daniel 3:16-17, Shadrach, Meshach and Abed-Nego answered and said to the King, "O Nebuchadnezzar, we have no need to answer in this matter. If that is the case, our GOD whom we serve is able to deliver us from the burning fiery furnace, and He will deliver us from your hands O King.*

When we were children, if my mother wanted to tell us about God and His power, this was also one of the chapter she drew her messages from. I grew up knowing Daniel in the lion's den, the three Hebrew boys and Jonah in bell of a fish. The Power God.

The plot against Daniel, *Daniel* 6: 1-9, *It pleased Darius to set over the kingdom one hundred and twenty straps, to be over the whole Kingdom. And over these three governors, of whom Daniel was one, that satraps might give account to them, so the king would suffer no loss. Then this Daniel distinguished himself above the governors and satraps because an excellent spirit was in him: and the king thought to set him over the whole realm. So the governors and the satraps thought to find some charges against Daniel concerning the kingdom: but they find no charge or fault, because he was faithful: nor was there any errors or fault found in him. Then these men said, "We shall not find any charges against this Daniel unless we find it against him concerning the law of his God. So these governors and satraps thronged before the king and said to him, ,"King Darius live forever! All the governors of the kingdom, the administrators and satraps, the counsellors and advisors have consulted together to establish a royal statute and to make a firm decree that whoever petition any* **god** *or any man for thirty days except you, O king, shall be cast into the den of lions. Now O king establish the decree and sign and the writing, so that it cannot be changed, according to the law of*

Medes and Persians, which does not alter. Therefore King Darius signed the written decree.

Daniel in lion's den, *Daniel 6 :11, Then these men assembled and found Daniel praying and making supplications before his God.*

V13, So they answered, before the King, "That Daniel, who is one of the captives from Judah does not show due regard for you, O King, or for the decree that you have signed, but make his petition three times a day."

V14,And the king when he heard these words was greatly displeased with himself and set his on Daniel to deliver him and he laboured till the going down of the sun to deliver him.

V15, Then these men approached the king and said to him , "Know, O king, it is the law of Medes and Persians that no decree or statute which the king establishes may be changed.

V16, So the king gave the command and they brought Daniel and cast him into the den of lions, but the King spoke to Daniel saying, "Your **God** *whom you serve will continually, He will deliver you.*

V17, Then a stone was brought and laid on the mouth of the den, and the King sealed it with his signet ring and with the signets of his lords, that the purpose concerning Daniel might not be charged.

Daniel saved from Lion's den, *Daniel 6:18-23, Now the King went to his palace and spent the night fasting: and not musicians were brought before him. Also his sleep went from him.*

V19, Then King arose very early in the morning and went in haste to the den of the lions.

V20, And when the King came to the den he cried out with a lamentation voice to Daniel, the King spoke saying to Daniel, "Daniel, servant of the living God, has your God whom you serve continually been able to deliver you from the lions?"

V21, Then Daniel said to the King, "O King live forever.

V22, My God sent His angel and shut the lion's mouth, so they have not hurt me, because I was found innocent before Him and also O King, I have done no wrong before you."

V23, Then the King was exceedingly glad for and commanded that they should take Daniel up out of the den. So Daniel was taken up out of the den and no injury whatever was found on him, because he believed in his God.

Jonah in belly of a fish;

Jonah 1:15-17, So they picked up Jonah and threw him into the sea, and the sea ceased from its raging. Then the men feared the Lord exceedingly, and offered sacrifice to the Lord and made vows. Now the Lord had prepared a great fish to swallow Jonathan. And Jonah was in the belly of the fish three days and three nights.

Jonah's prayer,

Jonah 2:1, Then Jonah prayed to the Lord his God from the fish's belly and said, I cried out to the Lord because of my afflictions and He answered me, "Out of the belly of Sheol I cried and you heard my voice.

Jonah 2:10, So the Lord spoke to the fish and it vomited Jonah into the dry land.

This takes me to the experience my son and I, had when him and I, went to Uganda to see my father. He was eight years old at that time. Him, my niece and I, were going to see my nephew at University, and as we waited for tax, they all happened to be full! I mean fully- packed! I decided that we turn back and go home but my niece insisted that we use boda-boda (motorcycles!) What? I had heard and seen bad stories due to dangerous driving and those motorcycles men, God help them, they do not to respect that big car! My niece is used to ride on motorcycle. But before I sat on it, I had already started worshipping God. Before I knew it my niece had gone together with my son! I to, sat on it and followed. For the whole journey I did not keep quiet. I worshipped, it's like I was in the church. I was afraid to look where we were going, I did not want to imagine ....! I said to myself, I must face the other side and keep up with worship but the man thought something was wrong with me, he asked, are you alright? I sang until. I couldn't wait to reach our destination! Thank God we reached but I did not know that my son in front of us was giving it to them, my niece said, Auntie, this Isaiah prayed psalm 91 all the way, he would pray, finished and repeat it again and again. But as my son prayed psalm 91, she and the driver were laughing! I said, that is what we eat. They were shocked, how can he know it all in his head! *Don't joke with psalm 91!*

Psalm 91, safety of abiding in the presence of God:

V1, He who dwells in the secret place of the Most High, shall abide in the shadow of the Almighty.

V2, I will say of the Lord, "He is my Refuge and Fortress, my God in Him I will trust.

V3, Surely He will deliver me from the snare of the fowler and from the deadly pestilence.

V4, He shall cover me with His feathers and under His wings, I shall take refuge. His truth shall be my shield and buckler.

V5, I shall not be afraid of the terror by night nor of the arrow that flies by the day.

V6, Nor of the pestilence that walks in darkness, nor of the destruction that lays waste at noon day.

V7, A thousand shall fall my side and ten thousand at my right hand but it shall not come near me.

V8, Only with my eyes I shall look and see and the reward of the wicked.

V9, Because I have made the Lord who is my refuge, even the Most High my habitation.

V10, North evil shall befall me, nor shall any plague (any disaster) come near my dwelling.

V11, For He shall ***give*** *His* ***angels*** *charge* ***over me*** *to* ***keep me*** *in* ***all my ways****.*

V12, They shall bear me (lift me) up in their hands lest I dash my food against a stone.

V13, I shall tread upon the lion and the cobra,the young lion and the serpents I shall trample them under foot.

V14, Because I have set my love upon Him, therefore, He will deliver me, He will set me on high because I have known His name.

V15, I shall call upon Him and He will answer me, He will be with me in trouble, He will deliver me and honour me.

V16, With long life He will satisfy me and show me His salvation.

Amen.

Lastly my testimony during COVID-19

Divine intervention,

I just don't want to take this lightly, what happened to me in March is not something to take for granted! It was so scary though I was not scared or moved! From the beginning I had already made up mind that I was not going to be shaken by this corona virus. I remember someone calling me from Uganda (my village) with panic but I said to him, we are OK! In fact I told him while laughing as if it was funny, and said, me I'm a stone, this corona virus will not move me. I said, if you don't asked me about it or tell me about I will not know that it's there because I did not put my mind on it. I said if it hears me coming, it will shift so that I could pass. I know it sounds arrogant but that is how I made up my mind to face it. I said, it can never rule! And my uncle in Uganda was emailing me now and then but my answer was, we are fine. Never took a test but I think, COVID-19, knocked at my door but it knocked on a wrong address! I did not go to hospital but I had every symptoms! I refused to tell anyone how I was feeling because I thought I would get many advices. In fact people who called to check on us just to find out how we were doing I told them that my son and I, were all fine. It was like a secret but for my own good. My medicine was Worship and to read Bible. My house was covered in worship. How it started, early March one Saturday my son woke up with such a horrible a cough! I admit that at that time I was still blind about corona virus. But it was rather annoying! I took him to the GP but he was not seen because we were late. We kept using our lemon, honey and garlic. And inhaling hot water (steam) Me I knew it was just a cough because before this COVID-19, people suffered coughs and flues, but when I called the school to report him absent I was told keep him at home fourteen days! Why? They explained! Anyway I kept him home treating a cough, then miraculously he was healed. I did not understand this but in my dream I saw our Pastor carrying my son on his back, in the dream we were in the Church and I could hear myself speaking *John 1:1, out loud, from the beginning there was a word, a word was with God and a word was God!* I thought it was on 11th March when I had that dream but when I checked properly, it was on Tuesday 17th March. I rewinded a week or two when I had headaches, a friend helped me because I was not able to drop my son to school. One Monday morning as I went to buy paracetamol and it was no where to be found! Every where I went, I went in super market just near me, and shops shelves were almost empty! I asked a lady, could you please show me where to get paracetamol? She looked at me and said, which planet do you come from? Within me I said, how rude! She went on to tell me that People were buying because in three months corona virus is going to be worse! I answered, says who? Well people are going to be badly affected buy this corona! She said, I asked again, says who? Then I told her, well, I'm saying no to that! It will not become worse! I only asked for paracetamol but I got to much information. The following day I went to buy toilet paper but shops were almost empty. Then I heard again, people are getting ready for corona virus! Getting ready! Again I said, says who? This time I spoke to myself and said, well it will not become worse for us, I said, are they prophesying or not? Anyway they say that if you can't beat them, you join them. I picked as much because I have a boy to feed. As if I knew, Thursday 19th that March, I was! My head was on fire, I was coughing, but I was drinking lemon, garlic and honey in warm water. I would just peel a lemon and eat it as if I was eating orange! My hair dresser was coming in my house to fix my hair but I told her, my son gave me a cough please don't come I don't want you to have it. I said will be patient until I'm clear. My only concern was my son, in the spirit I did not see corona in my body but my chest was hot, my shoulders were paining me, something would squeeze stomach so badly! I had suffered soar throat, something was on my throat, I could feel but I couldn't cough it out! I was taking paracetamol but mostly that home remedy, my lemon mixture with warm water. I was thirsty every minute, I needed a drink! I lost appetite, I couldn't eat food, I craved for Orange juice so I had this Ugandan fever but it was a coincidence! I said I have lived in UK nineteen years but I had never suffered a fever like this! My legs we shaking, but I said, corona virus, you are on a wrong address! As if it could hear me. I asked my son to lay his hands on me and to pray for me. I did not want to show him that I was very sick! But he said, Mummy will not died, she will live to take care of me. I stood in the kitchen and worshipped, I had You tube on, I sang this song, it say, *and I will not be* ***silent*** *I will I, will always worship you, as long as I'm breathing, I will always worship you, here is my worship, all of my worship,*

Father, receive my worship, all of my worship. Whoever wrote this song, I thank you! Because it became my medicine. People please do not joke with worship, worship carries power I just can't explain. And you have to read this Bible, I remember that all time even without corona virus, *psalm 91, psalm 23, psalm 12, Psalm 27 and Lords prayer,* these five have been weapons and food some how, it is a must! Next time you read these psalms, you will see that it was as if the one who wrote them, wrote them for a time like this! So it was too late for corona virus because I had already been eating. And there was another song in my local dialect, that song carries positive prophecy that I also stood on. I also tried to sing but at the end I couldn't, I was shivering too much. In bed it felt as it was winter. Even a dressing gown was not enough! I remember trying to make a phone call but I couldn't speak, I dropped the phone on the table because my chest was very hot. When I couldn't read Bible any more because of pain I decided to put on audio Bible but something told me to play my Pastor's messages, I was listening to his messages, thank God I had some CDs. In the night I would put my Pastor's CD message in the living room, then put audio Bible in the corridor and then I would put worship songs in my bedroom. That weekend one night my head became to painful, I can't explain the feeling! It was as if I could smell it! Then I remembered that I could cool my forehead with cold water, I went to the bathroom, soaked the face towel with cold and pressed it on my forehead. I rubbed vicks (pain balm) I felt as if I did not have the head because pain was too much that I could not feel it, but I knew God could heal me, for some reason I did not want to call ambulance to come and carry me to hospital! I said, what about my child! Then I put on my worship and slept, I could feel that my upper part of the body was different, I was trying to breathe, forcing myself to breathe, very strange! As I slept that Sunday, I had a dream, first my late father walked into my bedroom and called me to follow him but it was if I was back in Uganda. I followed my dead father, as I walked with him, I met my late mother also. For some reason my father and I sat somewhere on a black bench, when we got up he walked as if he was leading me into the banana plantation, down in the valley, I can *even* see the place. Then at that moment my Pastor appeared from nowhere and snatched me, and my father went alone. I did not follow my father any more, instead I started walking with my Pastor but I said, what is my Pastor doing in my village?! Him and I walked, he was wearing white African attire and he looked very, very handsome! When we reached somewhere in a town centre he sat on green grass! So I, sat with him but I had a desire to touch my pastor's feet, he removed his shoes and I knelt down and touched his feet. Then he asked me to bring anointing oil, he poured oil on me and Immediately him and I, were now in London, in the church. Then he said, everyone, bring your anointing oil, in my dreams I could see everyone in church running to get anointing oil, and everyone being anointed. I could actually see our Pastor standing at the altar anointing people in the church. It was at that time that I woke up from sleep. Waking up from sleep that morning I could not feel any pain, every discomfort disappeared, I could breathe properly, headache was completely gone so I was healed in that dream. It was a Divine intervention. *Thank you Jesus!* I kept on telling whoever called to check on us that my son and I, were fine. Then on Easter, that weekend again my uncle's wife called from Uganda to check on us, and I decided to tell her the story. She kept quiet for some time, then she said, I'm shocked! I said don't, be because God healed me. Why did you not tell us? She asked, I said, because I knew people would have made me to panic and I did not want to hear negative. You know! Betty, we have been worried about you, we called you daily and you chose to keep quiet! I said, imagine if I had told you that I had corona virus symptoms! She said, I would have been scared. I said and that is why I kept quiet. I kept on telling you people that we were fine, so it was! I told her, if corona virus is creeping and it finds me reading my Bible it can't stay. Then following day on Easter Sunday my elder sister called, I also told her the same thing but I added, I couldn't see my son my son left behind without a mother. Even to go to hospital I was asking myself were would he be? My sister said, But even if it had happened, Isaiah would have not suffered but I said to her, God forbid! I remember when all this corona virus started, my son prayed, he said, God I will not let me lose my parents, as well as praying for everyone. He prayed for his teachers in his school, and all the children in school. I remember one of my son's prayer: *please God, help us, let churches reopen again for gathering, so we may not have to stay at home on Sundays. Let schools reopen again and please God, help my daddy not to get this corona virus, In Jesus' name, and I said, Amen. Every now and then I would see him praying for his father! On 21st March* he came again and *said, this corona virus might have made the Church buildings to be closed but it has not closed the Bible. The Bible will remain open and we are yet to defeat this virus!*

About the author

Meet the author with no education; Betty Amiina, I was born and raised in Uganda but now I live in United Kingdom. God has blessed me with a wonderful son, Isaiah Wisdom Mujuni. I introduce myself as the author without school education, but that did not stop me from becoming what God created me to be. Yes it could have taken time, but better late better than never! I refused to be ruled by a life without education. My studies, I studied up primary seven back in that rural village. It's so funny that I have taken Bible to be that teacher whom I should have had! I have written over four hundred songs in English to the glory of God. God created me to worship Him, to give Him glory. He cannot really praise Himself. I discovered that the reason God made me was for His own pleasure. I remember a voice telling me in a dream in, I give you the handwriting of the holy sprit! I may not have understood the dream but I received it! It had taken a long time for me to forgive my father for not giving me that education when I was a child. Back then I remember that I wanted education so well, my mother was fighting hard to support me but she couldn't. I remember that one time while still in Uganda hatred crept into my heart and I felt like I hated my father, just for refusing me education. I tried hard to tell myself that I loved my father but it was hard! Back in Uganda I remember asking myself this question, Betty, for how long will you continue to blame your father for what he did not do? My consolation was, at least he gave birth to me. He could have chosen not to, but still it was hard to forgive him. Then one time after many years of living in UK, I sat down and I spoke these words to myself, I said, daddy, for everything you have ever done to me, I have forgiven you. It's like he was sitting beside me, I felt so good in my heart, I was not feeling heavy any more! At that moment I felt my Windows were opened and God could now hear me. To my experience no doubt, there is a blessing which is attached to a father. After settling that matter I turned to God and asked Him to be my teacher, one night I had another dream, in that dream I was reading, on the table, there was a lamp and I saw a finger running through pages. It was in that dream that I heard the voice, I have given the gift of writing! God is the best teacher. After fighting hard for many years, I don't know if it is out of disappointment or not but I decided to be intentional, on purpose. It's as if I said, OK, let me see who has power over me, education or God!

Lightning Source UK Ltd.
Milton Keynes UK
UKHW052039061120
372956UK00005B/373